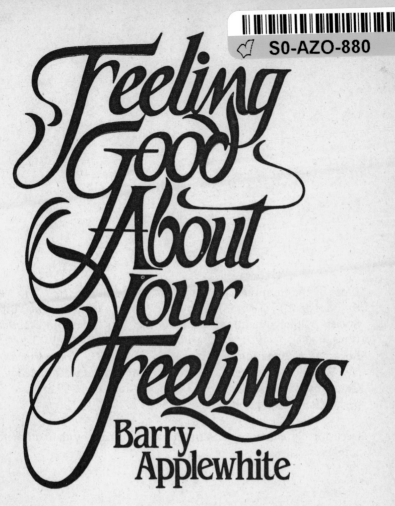

Feeling Good About Your Feelings

Barry Applewhite

While this book is designed for the reader's personal enjoyment and profit, it is also intended for group study. A leader's guide is available from your local Christian bookstore or from the publisher at $2.95

VICTOR BOOKS

a division of SP Publications, Inc.

WHEATON. ILLINOIS 60187

Offices also in Fullerton, California • Whitby, Ontario, Canada • Amersham-on-the-Hill, Bucks, England

Most of the Scripture quotations in this book are from *The New International Version,* © 1978 by The New York International Bible Society. Other quotations are from the *New American Standard Bible* (NASB), © 1960, 1962, 1963, 1968, 1971, 1972, 1973 by the Lockman Foundation, La Habra, California; *The Jerusalem Bible* (JB), © 1966 by Darton, Longman & Todd, Ltd. and Doubleday & Company, Inc.; and the King James Version (KJV). All are used by permission of the publishers.

Occasionally, portions of Scripture are italicized by the author for emphases.

Recommended Dewey Decimal Classification: 200.19 or 152.42
Suggested subject heading: EMOTIONS AND THE CHRISTIAN

Library of Congress Catalog Card Number: 80-51558
ISBN: 0-88207-792-9

VICTOR BOOKS
A division of SP Publications, Inc.
P.O. Box 1825 • Wheaton, Illinois 60187

Contents

Acknowledgments

Dr. Frank Wichern first encouraged me to understand
my emotions. I could not have done it without him!

Dr. Gene Getz helped me learn the art of writing
and guided me along the way.

Mrs. Mary Lou McNevin and Miss Mary Quinette gave
unselfishly of their talents in typing.

My warmest thanks to these four people!

Foreword

This is an exciting and stimulating book—for several reasons. First, it tackles head-on one of the most serious problems faced by many evangelical Christians—that of living in a separate world of ideas, concepts, and content. Putting it another way, many Christians tend to gravitate toward the cognitive aspects of Christianity and bypass the affective—the realm of feelings and emotions.

Don't misunderstand. Christianity at its very foundations *is* cognitive. It embraces a body of doctrine and beliefs, without which our faith would be purely existential. But Christianity is more than *what* we believe; it is also experiential and relational. God never intended for conversion and Christian growth to stop with the *head,* but to also involve the *heart.*

This book provides Christians with a strong biblical approach to this subject. And this is the second reason it is exciting. Many Christians react to their "cognitive only" heritage by immersing themselves in psychological literature and experiences—only to *overreact* and to bypass important scriptural input. Not so with this book. Without bypassing significant psychological insights, Barry begins each chapter with *what God says* and then sensitively applies that biblical truth in an experiential setting.

A third reason this book is exciting to me personally is because of my own ministry involvement with the author. Barry and I have shared the primary pastoral and teaching ministry at Fellowship Bible Church in Dallas for several years. During this time I have seen Barry courageously and with determination wrestle with the application of these concepts to his own life. At one time classifying himself as a "disciplined, perfectionistic and quite unemotional" person, he openly and honestly describes his personal journey into the realm of emotions.

Prayerful consideration of the principles evolved in this book will help you become a *total* person. It will also help you to *help others* grow. It is with enthusiasm that I recommend it to you.

Gene A. Getz
Dallas, Texas

**To my wife
Kay
who lovingly took new steps with me**

Preface

The Beginning: A Personal Journey

For me to write about emotions seems as likely as water running uphill. Educated as an engineer, I entered the field of nuclear power for five years with the Atomic Energy Commission. The profession fit my personality very well. I was disciplined, a perfectionist, and quite unemotional. I felt more at home with ideas than with people.

But my life's goals shifted and I left the field of atomic energy to enter seminary, where I received an excellent education in Bible knowledge and the training to communicate it to others.

While I was in seminary, my wife Kay and I joined Fellowship Bible Church, a ministry founded by Dr. Gene A. Getz and several Christian families in Dallas, Texas. Their goal was to develop a ministry which balances learning the Bible, developing close relationships, and communicating with non-Christians about Christ.

As time passed I joined the pastoral staff and became a teaching pastor at Fellowship Bible Church. But the relational aspect of this ministry eventually brought me face to face with a problem. I hadn't learned how to be comfortable in the world of emotions. People appreciated my sermons for the facts and logic, but some wondered about my real feelings and personality because I seldom let them show. They asked, "What is he *really* like?" Then came the breakthrough.

With a small group of church leaders and their wives, my wife and I became aware of our emotions and how to talk about them. Some sessions brought pain, but a strong bond of love developed that holds our group together.

The impact of this group experience launched me into a serious study of what writers in the Bible say about emotions. I wanted answers to some crucial questions. Why do people repress emotions? Why are they unaware of this important part of their personalities? Are emotions such as anger, sorrow, and anxiety sinful? If emotions are sinful under some circumstances and acceptable to God under others, how can a Christian know the difference? Does God have emotions? If not, how can He really understand us? Some answers to these questions surprised me.

I now think that one of the most neglected areas in an average Bible-teaching church is *relational* Christianity. And the basic reason for this neglect is a failure to recognize the importance of a proper expression of *emotions* in relationship with one another. I say *proper expression* because feelings need to be expressed in harmony with biblical principles. (I will use *feelings* and *emotions* interchangeably, although psychologists use *feelings* to mean our subjective experience of emotions.) Each Christian needs a basis for evaluating, controlling, and expressing emotions in a way that will build up the body of Christ. God has given us such a basis in His inerrant Word. As Christians we must look to the Bible as our final authority on the subject of emotions and their expression. This is what this book is about.

Like Father,
like Son

Centuries before the time of Christ, near the Greek city of Sparta, a young boy saw his teacher approaching on the path ahead. Fear gripped him.

At the age of seven, the boy had been taken from his home to enter a lifelong process of harsh military training. He had been taught to live off the land and even to plunder Spartan farms for food—and to hide every trace of emotion. Now a stolen fox squirmed to escape his grip as the boy considered the grim consequences of getting caught. In a desperate act he stuffed the wild fox under his cloak.

In keeping with Spartan custom, the teacher questioned the boy at length. As he calmly responded to his teacher's questions, the fox was gnawing and tearing at the boy's unprotected body, killing him. But his face never betrayed a hint of pain or fear. He had been trained well. Finally the boy, a model of Spartan discipline, fell dead at his teacher's feet.

Many evangelical Christians would make admirable Spartans! As a group we have even gone beyond the cultural standards which encourage us to hide our emotions. Covering up feelings has become an unwritten article of our Christian faith.

Almost all of *my* Christian life embodied the Spartan

syndrome until I began to ask myself some tough questions: How had I managed to live for over 30 years without fully realizing that emotions constitute a fundamental part of a person? How could I earn three degrees, including one in theology, without noticing how much writers of the Bible say about emotions? I concluded that I had systematically filtered out emotions as I studied the Bible and observed life.

When my wife and I joined a small group and interacted with four other couples for 11 weeks, the experience profoundly changed me. First, I was motivated to begin a serious search for biblical answers to some important questions: Does God have emotions? Does He *feel* anger, sorrow, joy, and other emotions? As I pulled many theology books from my shelves, I discovered again and again that these questions were not answered. I was shocked at the silence. Only rarely did these writers even mention the idea of God having emotions. How could such an important matter have been neglected? To find the answers, I sought help from a large seminary library. A fascinating story unfolded.

A Jewish Philosopher

The story begins about A.D. 10 when Philo Judaeus, an influential Jewish philosopher and student of Greek philosophy in Alexandria, Egypt, wrote a commentary on the Old Testament. Philo used Greek philosophy to write off all the Old Testament passages describing God's emotions. When he read statements in the Old Testament, such as: "the Lord was grieved . . . and His heart was filled with pain" (Gen. 6:6), he saw these verses through the filter of Greek philosophy which taught that a *god could not feel*. Obviously, God *felt* something about man's sin. Human behavior had an emotional impact on God. But Philo explained away the plain words of passages describing the Lord's emotions by saying that such a humanized description of God was merely a "crutch for our weakness." Thus, Philo influenced his successors with this type of philosophy.

Christian Theologians

Theologians of the early Christian church were influenced by the same precepts of Greek philosophy that had swayed Philo This affected their interpretation of the Bible—at least through the fourth century. During this crucial period, Christian theologians formulated church doctrine on God's nature Unfortunately, the questions regarding God's emotions were settled in their minds, and in the minds of future theologians, using the fallacious ideas of Greek philosophy. For instance, the famous *Westminster Confession of Faith,* which strongly influenced English and American theology, states, "There is but one only living and true God, who is . . . *without* body, parts, or *passions*" (italics mine, II.1, 1648).

To say that God is "without passions" means He cannot experience emotions as we know them. To this day, many evangelical theologians do not treat the subject of God's emotions. Some do describe God as having a rational, premeditated love for lost mankind and righteous angeɪ toward sin. But even these "God-felt" emotions seem quite different from our own, and many evangelical Christians do not think of God experiencing emotions as we do. That's exactly what *I* thought before I started digging.

When my theology books failed me, I turned to the Bible, ready to let God's Word speak for itself.

Divine Nature

Some people partially discount the emotions expressed by Jesus by saying that they emerge from His human nature and not from His divine nature. Such an argument fails when we see that the emotions Jesus expressed do not differ from the variety of God's emotions as recorded in the Old and New Testaments.

The Bible clearly shows us that Jesus experienced the emotions of anger, distress, sorrow, disappointment, frustra·tion, amazement, love and compassion, joy and delight. If the Son of God experienced such feelings without sin, then certain kinds of our emotions must be acceptable (even pleasing) to God.

1. Sorrow. Surprisingly, one of the first feelings ascribed to God is sorrow. God felt sad because man, His greatest creation, degenerated into sinful behavior. In this book we shall refer to this condition as *indwelling sin* or the *sinful nature.* We read, "The Lord was *grieved* that He had made man on the earth, *and His heart was filled with pain"* (Gen. 6:6).

Jesus frequently had to face human sin and opposition and He felt sorrowful and disappointed when He spoke of Jerusalem's sinful unbelief: "How often I have longed to gather your children together, as a hen gathers her chicks under her wings, but you were not willing!" (Luke 13:34)

2. Frustration and anger. These feelings emerge from God's statements that He has "no pleasure" in Israel's "meaningless offerings." He calls their incense "detestable" and says He "cannot bear" their worship meetings. "They have become a burden to Me" says the Lord. "I am *weary* of bearing them" (Isa. 1:14, see also vv. 11-13).

God says His anger will be aroused against those who take advantage of widows and orphans (Ex. 22:22-24). Israel's complaining and Moses' griping also aroused God's anger (Num. 11).

When we read Mark 3, we find that Jesus was surrounded by His enemies. He asked them if the Law of Moses would allow Him to heal a crippled man on the Sabbath. But because of their uncaring, stubborn hearts, they refused to answer. Jesus not only felt angry but deeply distressed over the hardened hearts of the Pharisees. Their observance of petty, man-made rules meant far more to them than the years of human anguish caused by that man's withered hand.

Jesus also experienced the feeling of frustration. I think mothers of small children will particularly identify with this emotion, and as a father, I can better accept feelings of frustration with my three small children when I see that Jesus experienced frustration *without sin.* The biblical account of the incident begins when a man takes his demon-possessed son to Jesus' disciples, but they are unable to help him. Then the father takes his son to Jesus who says, "O unbelieving and perverse generation, . . . how long shall I stay with you, and *put up with you?*" (Luke 9:41)

3. Love and compassion. An example of God's emotions from the New Testament shows how God felt before Jesus came to redeem man. Notice how differently the verse strikes you when you imagine God feeling as He acts: "For God so *loved* the world, that He gave His one and only Son, that whoever believes in Him shall not perish but have eternal life" (John 3:16).

Having one son myself, I am struck by God's feelings. He didn't send Christ to die for you and me just because it was part of some grand plan formed before the world began. He did it because He really cared and still cares about us with feelings of love and compassion.

A moving example of Christ's compassion occurred as He approached the little town of Nain. He saw a widow leading the funeral procession for burial of her only son. Jesus' "heart went out to her" because of her profound loss (Luke 7:12-13). In His great compassion for this woman, Jesus raised her son from the dead and transformed her grief into joy.

4. Amazement. It had never occurred to me that Jesus could experience amazement until I read of His response to a Roman centurion's faith. This officer was convinced that Jesus could heal his servant from a great distance by simply speaking a command. Jesus "marveled at him" and commended the man's "great faith" before the crowd (Luke 7:9, NASB).

5. Joy and delight. God can also feel joyful and delighted. Zephaniah speaks of the Lord taking great delight in His people and rejoicing over them with singing (Zeph. 3:17). One woman responded to this by saying, "I've always thought about the angels and redeemed people in heaven singing—but God singing? He's supposed to just sit there!" The familiar Parable of the Prodigal Son (actually about the loving father) also pictures the father's joy in rich colors of deep feeling (Luke 15:32).

God has revealed Himself as Someone with real emotions. He wants us to know that He feels, He cares, and He can be emotionally moved. Similarly, to miss the emotional dimension of Christ's personality is to create an other worldly Jesus. He was human *and* divine, and yet He was not a stranger to emotions.

A Sensitive Heart

You may reason that Jesus could experience emotions without sinning because He is God, while it's impossible for us to experience feelings like sorrow, distress, and anger without sinning. But the Bible refutes this line of reasoning with the example of Paul, the brilliant and forceful apostle to the Gentiles. Paul, a human being just like us (Acts 14:15), displayed anger and sorrow without apparent concern for doing so.

Paul spoke touchingly of the "great sorrow and unceasing anguish" in his heart because so many Jews were cut off from Christ by unbelief (Rom. 9:2-4). We can also hear a well-meaning Christian interrupting Paul and saying, "Hold it, Paul! What's the matter with you? Are you out of fellowship? If you are a Christian, is it right for you to be feeling sorrowful?"

Real, spiritual believers shouldn't feel this way, should they? Paul apparently thinks they can. In fact, he wrote the first Letter to the Corinthians "out of great distress and anguish of heart and with many tears" (2 Cor. 2:4). Paul not only had a brilliant mind but also a sensitive heart.

Paul's anger glowed with fierce intensity in his Letter to the Galatians. He expressed his feelings toward the church by twice calling them "foolish" (Gal. 3:1-3). Paul had led these people to Christ, but they were being subverted by false teachers.

If your anger detector didn't register over Paul calling the Galatian believers "foolish," I'll bet it leaps off the table as you read how Paul felt about the false teachers! These men came in after Paul and taught the Galatians that they must be circumcised and keep the Law of Moses, in addition to having faith in Jesus. Speaking in relation to their circumcision doctrine, Paul said, "As for those agitators, I wish they would go the whole way and emasculate themselves!" (Gal. 5:12) Paul proved to us that human emotions and service for God can go hand in hand.

In God's Image
Many awesome truths are taught in the Bible, but few can match the grandeur of God saying, "Let Us make man in Our image, and in Our likeness" (Gen. 1:26). I am convinced that *man has emotions because God has emotions*. Our emotions are a God-intended, God-created capacity for feeling! I believe that some Christians (and especially *men* with personalities like my own) have traded this view of emotions for the ancient Stoic view that emotions demean us and must be controlled with an iron will.

Without any doubt, man's emotional life was affected by the fall of mankind into sin. But not even sin can erase the divine basis and origin of human emotions. Believers bear God's image, not only as human beings, but also as those in whom the Spirit works, as He conforms us to the image of Christ.

Once in a great while, a brave person will break the cultural taboos which prevent the frank expression of emotions. About two years ago, a close friend made a statement in an elders' meeting in the presence of 35 other men. He told them that I was the best friend he had ever had and that he loved me very much. His bold statement struck me like a tidal wave, breaking down my defenses against emotions. I was deeply touched. I'm quite sure that my Father in heaven *felt* pleasure with our emotions.

Emotions and You
1. Do I accept emotions? You may find yourself apologizing

to others for your emotional moments. Perhaps you excuse yourself by saying, "I'm a very emotional person." Would it not be more appropriate to explain to others how you feel rather than trying to explain your feelings away? Should you not accept what God has created in you—the capacity to feel?

2. *Do I think of emotions as sinful?* Some people think of many emotions as inherently sinful. If you are fearful, sad, angry, uncomfortable, or frustrated, does that always mean that you are sinning? I think not!

We must be cautious in accepting the opinion of well-meaning people who would see or experience such emotions and conclude that the answer is "getting back into fellowship with God" or "just giving these feelings to the Lord." Such emotions are not necessarily sinful.

3. *Do I cover up emotions?* Many of us restrain or cover up our emotions because we don't want to lose face. It is a matter of pride or fear. To show our feelings is to betray human weakness. Instead of being truly human, we try to conform to a false standard created by our contemporary culture.

An Opportunity to Change Your Life

The following will help you evaluate your approach to emotions in yourself and others. During the next week, watch carefully for signs of covering up your emotions and then evaluate why this is happening. Look for the following symptoms:

- cutting off communication with someone;
- resisting an impulse to cry, laugh, scream, or any other *extreme* of emotional expression;
- working to keep facial expression in tight control (keeping a *poker* face);
- talking only theoretically about ideas or issues rather than how you feel about them;
- feeling physically bad (for instance, headache, tight neck muscles), after someone puts pressure on you or has had a conflict with you;

- thinking frequently about what you should have said to someone (or what you want to say next time).

2
Learning to Live with Anger

Of all the emotions that have troubled me as a Christian and a pastor, anger bothers me most. For years I denied that I was angry. *Christians shouldn't be angry,* I thought, *and certainly not pastors!* Ignoring anger in myself was enhanced by my tendency to pay attention to facts and to give little attention to feelings.

As with any person, my emotions at times became so intense that they could no longer be suppressed or ignored. At that point I would change tactics. I would grit my teeth, withdraw from the person provoking my anger, and wait for the anger to go away. Times without number I would use this silent burn technique on my wife. I even considered such an approach spiritual because it took so much control to wait for the anger to go away!

The long-term destructiveness of anger, which many believers either deny or keep within them, is now a widely held opinion. Psychiatrists Dr. Frank Minirth and Dr. Paul Meier state, "Over and over in the literature on the subject, depression is described as anger turned inward" (*Happiness Is a Choice,* Baker, p. 99).

Anger within us does not simply go away. It festers within us like an infected wound. It causes depression on a massive national scale and Christians are not beyond its grasp. In fact, Minirth and Meier state that, "A *majority* of Americans suffer from a serious, clinical depression sometime during their lives" (*Happiness Is a Choice,* p. 20).

These bleak facts about depression shattered my own sense of security about my way of handling anger. I had always thought ignoring my anger (or not venting it on others) put me in a fail-safe position. But repressed anger harms me and ultimately harms others too. In spite of my previous deep suspicions about all forms of anger, I was forced to reexamine the Bible for principles about anger.

Five Biblical Principles

Five principles emerged as I studied anger throughout the Bible. The first principle shocked me a bit.

1. Anger in itself is not necessarily sinful. This principle flatly contradicts the view held by many evangelical Christians. It seems to cut across the grain of their spiritual assumptions. But Paul destroys the theory that all anger is sin when he says, "'In your anger do not sin': Do not let the sun go down while you are still angry, and do not give the devil a foothold" (Eph. 4:26-27). The translators who worked on the *New International Version* of the Bible softened the literal meaning of the original Greek text of verse 26 which reads, *"Be angry* and do not sin."* In actuality, there are *two* commands in verse 26. The fact that the translators render only one as a command seems to reflect our general discomfort with anger. The point Paul is making is that when we become angry, the biggest challenge we face is to not express anger in sinful ways.

You may find these statements difficult to accept. I know that I have read this verse hundreds of times without being receptive to its literal meaning. However, we can be comfortable with such a concept when we realize that we are to be angry for the same reasons God becomes angry. (Much more will be said about this in chapter 3.)

Notice that Paul says, "Do not let the sun go down while you are still angry" (Eph. 4:26). According to first century Jewish thought, a day ended with sunset. So anger had to be dealt with urgently—not suppressed with all its destructive power. Almost 2,000 years ago, Paul gave this command which we now know inhibits depression. We as believers must deal with anger urgently to prevent "giving the devil a foothold" (Eph. 4:27). But the main potential for sin lies in our *expression* of anger and not necessarily in the emotion itself.

2. *People tend to express anger in sinful ways because of indwelling sin.* Expressing anger causes the most trouble. In our anger we *do* tend to sin because we have a sinful nature. And that nature always wants to take our emotions and twist them into sin.

James put his finger on the source of sinful expression when he said, "What causes fights and quarrels among you? Don't they come from your *desires* that battle within you?" (James 4:1) The word James used for *desires* is the Greek word from which we get our word *hedonism.* A hedonistic person seeks to satisfy his own desires; he sees pleasure as the highest goal of life. Jesus warns us about the sin nature when He refers to every form of evil as coming "from within, out of men's hearts" (Mark 7:21-23).

Man's nature was invaded by sin when Adam and Eve first disobeyed God. This nature pushes all of us toward the sinful expression of our anger. What we need is a counterforce to help us override our sinful nature, and such power can only be found in the Lord.

3. *The Holy Spirit and the Word of God make it possible to control the expression of our anger.* Without Scripture we would not know the causes of anger or the possibility of being angry apart from sin. The Word of God provides crucial insight for understanding anger and explains the power available to us to control anger.

God makes it possible for *every* believer to handle anger through the Holy Spirit. The Scriptures teach that every Christian has God's indwelling Spirit. In fact, if a person does not have the Spirit, then he is not a Christian (Rom. 8:9). Paul makes it clear that the Spirit can enable the Christian to manage anger when he says, "Live by the Spirit, and you will not gratify the desires of the sinful nature" (Gal. 5:16). In every Christian, conflict rages between the sinful nature and the indwelling Spirit, but the Spirit has the upper hand.

However, while the power of the Spirit is *available,* it is *not automatic.* We can only enjoy the benefits of this power by using our will. We must choose to do God's will as it stands revealed in His Word. As we decide to obey the Lord, the Spirit gives us adequate power. Thus Paul appeals to our wills with commands to serve God rather than sin (Rom. 6:11-14). Our freedom to make such a choice and carry it out depends upon the indwelling Spirit's power (Rom. 8:5-13). Peter also describes our capability as believers by saying, "His divine power has given us everything we need for life and godliness" (2 Peter 1:3).

But the danger we face from our sinful nature remains real, since at times we willingly cooperate with sin. We Christians often sin in expressing anger because we fail to make use of all the resources God has provided.

4. Since God holds us accountable for all our behavior, the control and resolution of anger must be our goal. Control of our anger is not optional. All of us believers will be held responsible for our behavior as it relates to the command given in Ephesians 4:26, "In your anger do not sin." Paul tells us in 2 Corinthians 5:10 that all of our actions will be evaluated at the Judgment Seat of Christ. As believers, we will not experience divine wrath in any form. However, negative consequences will come to us as a result of disobedient behavior. Paul is probably referring to a loss of reward which could have been ours.

Many people find it difficult to admit how frequently they feel anger. But whether we recognize it or not, some degree of anger arises frequently within all of us; so expressing and resolving our anger without sin takes on great importance.

5. Expressing and resolving anger demands a plan of action.

As soldiers in spiritual warfare (Eph. 6:10-17), we need a battle plan for anger including three stages: We must recognize anger, evaluate it spiritually, and resolve it without sin. (Evaluating and resolving anger will be treated in chapter 3.)

Recognizing Anger

Defining anger would help us recognize it, but anger is notoriously hard to define. Based on the discussion in both this chapter and the next one, *anger* could be defined as *an inclination toward aggressive behavior, against oneself or others, provoked by one's indwelling sin or by the sin of others.*

Recognizing anger takes more effort by some people than by others. In my own case I was trained to process facts, not feelings. The nature of my work as a nuclear engineer conditioned me to focus only on facts and actions. In essence, my supervisors told me to produce *results.* How I *felt* about my work or my associates was unimportant. So emotions like anger were simply a distraction to me. They could not help me produce results.

As I have concentrated on developing emotional sensitivity, I have learned to recognize certain *anger signals*—

- disagreement or conflict with someone (even if no words are spoken to one another);
- our voices raised above a conversational level;
- a suddenly increased heart rate or breathing rate;
- a mental rehearsal of what I should have said or will say next time;
- a desire to punish someone, tell him off, or get revenge;
- frequent criticism of someone or self-criticism (which indicates anger toward oneself).

Now see if you can recall experiencing any of these anger signals in one of the following situations:

☐ Your husband or wife says, "I'm sorry," but soon does the same thing all over again.

☐ Someone at work or in the neighborhood says unkind things about you or a friend behind your back.

☐ Someone almost causes a car wreck by pulling out in front of you.

☐ You did something wrong and said to *yourself,* "You idiot! How could you have been so dumb?"

☐ You abruptly ended a conversation by walking off in a huff.

☐ You want to hit and hurt.

If you did not identify with some anger in at least three of these situations, then you are either under three years of age, dead, or highly unaware of your emotions!

Personality traits (no matter what causes them) have a great deal to do with becoming angry. Three personality traits are particulary significant in the case of anger: selfishness, perfectionism, and suspiciousness. Everyone has such traits at times, but look for persistent trends in your attitudes and behavior Ask yourself:

- Am I often selfish? Do others see selfishness in me? Does selfishness often cause my anger?

- Am I often perfectionistic? Do others consider me unreasonable in my standards for myself and others? Does this lead me to anger against myself and others?

- Am I often suspicious? Do I misinterpret people's motives? Do many actions by others seem to threaten me?

Significant relationships (such as with a close friend or a marriage partner) provide the primary setting for anger to occur. Husbands and wives often experience anger because they have *different expectations.* How about you? Mark those areas where you experience anger with your mate due to conflicting expectations or approaches—

☐ the priority of home and family in relation to work;

☐ the home and how clean and orderly it should be;

☐ the disciplining of the children;

☐ the frequency of sexual relations;

☐ the way to use money (level of debt, luxuries, saving credit);

☐ the amount and type of spiritual activities.

When we have learned to recognize anger-producing situations and their symptoms, we are on the way to evaluating and then resolving our anger.

A Personal Response
Read the Book of Esther and pick out every passage where anger influences the course of events. Then think about this question: What caused Haman's anger and how did it change his life?

Learning to Resolve Anger

Have you ever wondered why we use the word *mad* as a substitute for *angry?* It may be because *mad* has the implication of "being insane," and anger can relieve us of all reason. If you think this is overstating the case, consider this true story:

A Florida man was recently being held in custody awaiting bail for a *minor* offense. When he began shouting obscenities, the bailiffs hauled him quickly before the judge. "What seems to be the trouble?" asked the judge.

After another profane outburst, the judge sentenced the man to one year in jail for contempt of court.

"One year! Why don't you make it five?" the man shouted.

"Okay, five," said the judge sternly.

"You might just as well make it ten!" the man screamed in rage.

"Okay, ten years and $10,000," announced the judge.

Mercifully, the bailiffs hustled the prisoner back to jail before he could go for twenty. He had not learned how to resolve his anger and it robbed him of his senses.

A first step toward resolving anger is recognizing it. A second step is evaluating it.

Evaluating Anger

The Bible provides a frame of reference for evaluating anger.

Figure 1 pictures the two major facts that define man's basic nature. First, man was created in *the image of God,* which results in man having emotions just as God does. Second, man has indwelling sin (or a sinful nature) as a result of sin entering the human race through Eve yielding to Satan's temptation and Adam's subsequent sin. Indwelling sin may ultimately be traced back to Satan. To have a sinful nature does not mean that man does everything wrong or that he is as evil as he might be. But having it does mean that within him surge impulses toward greed, lust, selfishness, and covetousness.

$$
\text{God} \text{------} \underset{\text{God}}{\overset{\text{Image of}}{}} \longrightarrow \text{MAN} \longleftarrow \underset{\text{Sin}}{\overset{\text{Indwelling}}{}} \text{------} \text{Satan}
$$

Figure 1

When God encounters human sin, He becomes angry. The Bible confirms this hundreds of times. In His anger, God responds to human sin in two ways. He primarily responds with compassion, as shown by sending His Son to die for all sinners, so that they would never have to take God's anger on themselves. God sometimes reacts to human sin with vengeance and punishment. Everyone who refuses Christ as God's solution to sin is choosing God's anger instead. His anger is obviously appropriate or justifiable as He responds to human sin.

That's the key! Just as God becomes appropriately angry with human sin, we who are made in His image are capable of having the same emotional response of *positive anger* toward sin. Injustice, exploitation, disobedience, and mistreatment produce positive anger in us because we are made in God's image. For instance, most of us have seen football players become enraged because of the *injustice* of a bad call by a referee. Many people I know were angered recently by adherents of an Eastern religion who *exploited* a mentally retarded child by conning him into a contribution. In our church we experienced anger against child *abuse* as we prayed for a counselor who was dealing with six different cases of sexually abused children. Many Christians become angry when another believer ruins his own life by willfully *disobeying* God. Such anger in us is not sin!

On the other hand, because we all have sinful natures, anger can arise in us for the wrong reasons and then we experience *negative anger*. For example, I may become angry with someone simply because I didn't get my way. Such negative anger finds its roots in selfishness and ultimately in my sinful nature. It certainly does not come from God or from being made in His image. So anger within us can be categorized as either positive or negative. What many Christians need to hear is that *some anger is positive*.

When a Christian becomes angry, the immediate thought is, *I must be sinning since I am so angry*. The crucial step at that point is that this Christian should determine whether his anger has arisen (like God's) because of human sin or whether he feels angry because of his own indwelling sin. He will usually find that his anger consists partly of positive anger and partly of negative anger.

Resolving Anger

Our analysis of anger up to this point is summarized in figure 2. Another step is added in figure 3. Anger as an emotion which arises in us must be distinguished from the *expression* of that anger. Even positive anger can be expressed in a wrong way. I may see someone selling dangerous drugs to small children and become properly angry with human sin. But if I take a gun and kill the drug dealer, my positive anger has been expressed by sinning.

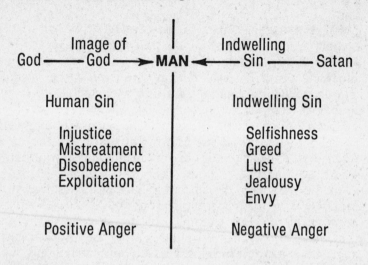

Figure 2

The other side of the story is that even negative anger can be resolved in a right way. After James traces negative anger to indwelling sin, he tells us how to resolve such anger by saying, "Submit yourselves, then, to God. Resist the devil, and he will flee from you. Come near to God and He will come near to you" (James 4:7-8).

Anger can be expressed in several ways. *Either kind of anger* can be acted out sinfully or with love and obedience to God. God has given us everything we need to handle the expression of anger through His Holy Spirit. Our task as believers is to decide to "live by the Spirit" (Gal. 5:16), by obeying God's commands in an anger crisis rather than following our sinful nature. When we use this frame of reference, Paul's strange-sounding command, "Be angry and do not sin," becomes clear. After recognizing anger we can evaluate it from a spiritual perspective and respond to it in a godly way.

Resolving positive anger. Examining how God resolves His holy anger against human sin can give us a pattern for resolving our positive anger. He first responds to human sin with

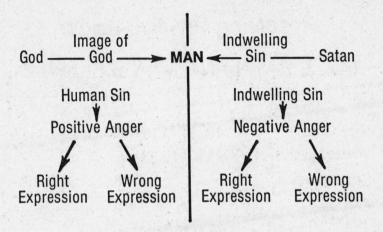

Figure 3

compassion, forgiveness, reconciliation, and communication.
God not only took action to eliminate His anger toward us, but
He also <u>communicated</u> with us. What if God had been angry
with us because of our sin all this time but had never told us?
What if God had never revealed our sin problem and His
solution in Jesus Christ? Even in the resolution of divine anger,
communication has played a major role, so the *necessity* of
communication in resolving human anger should not be
surprising.

God's second way of resolving His anger consists of
vengeance and punishment on those who continually insist on
rejecting His mercy. God does not want to deal with men using
wrath, but He will do so if He must (2 Peter 3:9).

Resolving our positive anger requires the same elements of
compassion that God uses in handling His anger against sin.
We are to exercise compassion, forgiveness, reconciliation,
and communication. Jesus spoke about this approach for
resolving anger when He said that if our brother has something
against us, we should seek reconciliation as a higher priority
than worshiping God (Matt. 5:23-24). In the preceding case,

Resolving Positive Anger

GOD'S PATTERN		MAN'S RESPONSE
Compassion Forgiveness Reconciliation Communication	**FIRST COMMANDED**	Compassion Forgiveness Reconciliation Communication
Vengeance Punishment	**SECOND PROHIBITED**	Inaction Vengeance Punishment (see exceptions)

Exceptions:

1. Parents may discipline children with love.
2. The church may discipline members with love.
3. Human government may punish citizens.

Figure 4

the other person is angry with us. However, Jesus also referred to the same basic process of reconciliation when we are angry with someone else (Matt. 18:15). Notice in Matthew 5, Jesus stresses the urgency of dealing with anger just as Paul does in Ephesians 4. When we resolve our positive anger as God does, we prevent sin and depression.

But here we hit a snag. What if we become angry with

someone quite remote from us? What if the president makes a tax proposal costing us $500, or a bad call in a TV football game gives our team a crucial defeat? We don't have the option of calling the president or the referee on the phone to seek reconciliation. But we can decide by an act of our wills to forgive in such cases. The Holy Spirit gives us ability as believers to forgive others; therefore, we should do *something* about our anger against remote people, by consciously deciding to forgive.

God's Word also informs us how *not* to resolve our positive anger. God condemns inaction, and forbids vengeance and punishment as expressions of positive anger. So Paul says, "Do not take revenge, my friends, but leave room for God's wrath, for it is written: 'It is Mine to avenge; I will repay,' says the Lord" (Rom. 12:19). Leaving punishment in the Lord's hands can be the mot difficult aspect of anger; though, in certain cases God permits us to take limited action as an expression of our positive anger against sin. The three main cases are—

- that parents may discipline children with love;
- that the church may discipline members with love;
- that governments may punish citizens.

Figure 4 summarizes how to resolve positive anger.

Resolving negative anger. God's Word also spells out our options for resolving negative anger. Figure 5 depicts what the writers of James 4 and Galatians 5 teach about this.

All of us struggle with self-centeredness, greed, lust, and covetousness—which are four basic expressions of indwelling sin. Each of these factors can cause negative anger. Our first goal is to change our minds about our behavior and resubmit ourselves to the rule of Christ in our lives. The Bible calls such a change "repentance." Repentance goes beyond the first change of mind that leads us to salvation through faith in Christ. Repentance also constitutes the believer's frequent need to change his mind and behavior before God. Again, the Holy Spirit provides every needed resource to make this change possible.

Resolving Negative Anger

```
Repentance
Submission to God        COMMANDED
Reconciliation
Communication
```

```
Inaction
Vengeance, Fits of rage   PROHIBITED
Attacking, Fighting
Hating, Quarreling
```

Figure 5

Summary of Steps in Managing Anger

1. *Recognition* of anger
2. *Evaluation* of anger:
   a. What are the reasons or causes behind the anger that I feel?
   b. What are the responses available?
   c. How do these causes and responses compare to the principles of God's Word?
3. *Resolution* of anger (either positive or negative):
   a. Leave vengeance to God!
   b. Seek reconciliation urgently—communicate in love!
   c. Use God's channels for any punishment which is required.
   d. Overall, let love and forgiveness guide.

Now or Later?

Anger can lead to sin and also to serious depression. How urgent it is that we learn to handle anger!

One of my favorite TV commercials sells oil filters. The auto mechanic in the ad wears black and looks like a mortician. There is an otherworldly atmosphere in the scene and behind the mechanic we can see a car being towed into his garage. In your heart you know it is a *dead* car. The mechanic/mortician holds an oil filter in his hands as he says, "You know, this little filter would have cost him $5, but now he'll have to pay $500. You've got your choice. You can pay me now *or* (with a respectful glance toward the dead car) you can pay me later." Anger affects us the same way. We can deal with it now or pay for it later.

Practice Makes Perfect

Use the following concepts to focus on your evaluation and resolution of anger:

1. Lots of people have arguments, which always involve anger, but few think back through the situation and their anger. Such thinking can pay big dividends. You may find a common pattern or theme which can then be changed.

Concentrate on the last argument or significant disagreement you had with someone.

I argued with—

- my mate;
- my children;
- my friend or neighbor;
- my boss or a co-worker;
- my teacher or another student;
- other.

(Note: If you never have arguments or sharp disagreements with anyone, then it is highly probable that you are repressing anger. Depression will present a greater danger in that case. Exploding with pent-up anger may also occur.)

My *anger* was caused by—

- prior behavior by the other person; mistreatment, injustice, exploitation, or disobedience;
- a threat to my position, self-esteem, income, or security;
- jealousy, envy, or competitiveness on my part.

(Compare your responses with figure 2 and answer below.)
My anger was—

- positive (i.e., caused by someone else's sin);
- negative (i.e., casued by my own sinfulness);
- a mixture of positive and negative.

My *purpose* in the disagreement was—

- to explain how I had been hurt or mistreated;
- to resolve the problem and make peace;
- to hurt back by name-calling, overstating ("You *always/never* do"), or even by hitting;
- to win; make him lose; put him in his place;
- other.

(Compare your responses with those in figures 4 and 5.)

After evaluating the argument, you may find that further action is needed to resolve positive and negative anger.

2. Do you allow your children the freedom to express their anger in appropriate ways? Some Christian parents think that *any* expression of anger is a sin which the rod will soon remove. Some expressions of anger in our children must be disciplined, but if we attack all expressions of our children's anger they will simply learn how to hide emotions. This is an excellent way to produce adults who cannot deal with anger. As adults we need to take special care with small children. With our help they need to learn how to articulate their feelings of anger in acceptable ways. When parents simply say to children, "We know that must have made you angry," small children gain tremendous reassurance because their parents understand what's happening inside them. (Feelings of anger toward parents can frighten small children and create guilt in them.

The best way to teach children to handle anger is to learn to manage it ourselves.

"Lord, I'm Angry with You!"

Pastors and their families share the same problems that other families feel—such as pressures at work. Often my family faces tensions in relation to the sermons I prepare. One Tuesday my seven-year-old daughter Nancy became quite sick with a stomachache. As she lay suffering on the couch, bad feelings were developing within her—and I don't mean physical feelings! When I stopped to check on her, she said, "I keep on praying to God to make me well and He just doesn't do *anything*!" These words flew from Nancy's mouth like a quick burst of machine gun bullets. They caught me quite by surprise In response I accepted her anger and tried to persuade her that God loves her even when He lets sickness strike. I'm glad I didn't say, "Nancy, we just can't talk that way or feel that way about God," because my turn to feel anger toward Him came next.

Since I must preach each week, I live or die by the quality of my last day of preparation. Fridays bring on a landslide of work to finalize my message before the first church service that night. In the same week of Nancy's illness, my wife Kay became violently ill, beginning on Thursday night before midnight (Kay was to show no improvement until 6 A.M. Friday morning.) After doing what little I could for her, I moved to another room to get my crucial rest for Friday. I was almost asleep when my one-year-old son woke up. For the first time in months, he decided to get up and play from midnight to 3 A.M. So I had plenty of time to think, but I didn't use it to prepare for my upcoming sermon. Instead I was saying, "Lord, what are You doing? You know I can't afford to have this happen now!" I felt quite angry with God. It was inconvenient for me that my wife was sick and my son was awake. How was I going to get my work done without rest? I didn't actually come out and say, "Lord, I'm angry with You!" but I think He got the message. Ironically, the sermon subject I had scheduled for Friday was, "Anger toward God."

Doesn't this happen to you too? Whether you actually tell Him so or not, don't you sometimes become angry with God? I feel safe in assuming your answer is yes. How can you and I handle such anger? Perhaps, more importantly, how will God respond to such anger? The Lord supplies some answers for us in His response to Jonah in the Bible.

Prelude to Anger

Few biblical characters can rival the brashness of Jonah. He lived during the reign of Jeroboam II (see 2 Kings 14:25), about 760 B.C. Assyria dominated the Middle East at this time and Israel was quite weak. God wanted Jonah to go to Nineveh, the capital city of the Assyrian Empire, almost 600 miles northeast of Jerusalem. But Jonah didn't want to go so he fled west to Joppa and sailed on the first westbound ship he could find. Jonah's plans were totally different from God's. The Lord used many circumstances, including a storm and a great fish, to bring Jonah back to the coast of Israel. Due to an experience at sea that almost took his life, Jonah realized that he could not escape from either God or the journey to Nineveh. God used an experience to change Jonah's mind—a strategy He was to use again.

We can certainly identify with some of the reservations Jonah must have felt. His message for the Assyrians was destined to be about as popular as cancer. And he proclaimed to them: "Forty more days and Nineveh will be destroyed" (Jonah 3:4).

Contrary to all of Jonah's expectations, the Ninevites humbled themselves before God and sought His mercy. From the lowest beggar to the king, the Assyrians put on sackcloth and declared a fast to ask the Lord for mercy.

Why the proud Assyrians repented so quickly and completely remains a mystery, although natural factors may have influenced their response. At this time Assyria's might had declined to the lowest level in years; before and after this period in history the empire had been and would be much stronger. Serious plagues and a total eclipse of the sun also occurred at about the same time. Such calamities, which deeply influenced the ancient mind, may have been God's instruments to bring the Assyrians literally to their knees. But whatever the cause, the people of Nineveh were converted to the Lord. And God changed his mind about the judgment He had declared through Jonah.

Jonah's Anger

Such a great day of salvation moves us with pleasure, but one person despised it—Jonah. Many preachers would give their own lives to convert 120,000 people, but Jonah was prepared to give his life to see the city destroyed. Read the record of Jonah's feelings: "But Jonah was greatly displeased and became angry" (Jonah 4:1). The Hebrew words translated in this verse as "Jonah was greatly displeased" literally mean "it was terribly evil to Jonah." Jonah considered the Lord's actions in saving Nineveh to be *evil.* And so Jonah felt great anger toward God. But why did Jonah think it was evil for a city to repent and be spared from destruction?

How easily we can get down on Jonah and assume a pious attitude: "Jonah shouldn't have acted that way," we say. While this is true, Jonah had reasons from a human viewpoint for his anger toward God. In chapter 3 we saw that injustice causes anger to arise in us, and from Jonah's perspective, God's mercy toward Nineveh was not just. Jonah's anger was partly due to the fact that Assyria was one of the most ruthless and bloodthirsty empires that the world had known. Consider this typical inscription from an Assyrian monarch ruling about a century before Jonah came to Nineveh:

I carried off their spoil and their possessions. The heads of their warriors I cut off, and I formed them into a pillar over against their city, their young men and their maidens I burned in the fire . . . I flayed (i.e. skinned alive) all the chief men who had revolted, and I covered the pillar with their skins (Jack Finegan, *Light From the Ancient Past,* Princeton University Press, p. 170).

The inscription continues but we'll stop before our stomachs rebel. Such inscriptions can be found many times in the annals of the Assyrian kings.

Nahum, the prophet, wrote *after* the time of Jonah when God did bring judgment on Nineveh. Nahum said, "Woe to the city of blood, full of lies, full of plunder, never without victims" (Nahum 3:1). Nahum later said that Nineveh's destruction would be celebrated by universal rejoicing because of her "endless cruelty" (Nahum 3:19).

There was much hatred in the ancient East for Assyria and its capital; Jonah and countless others wanted death for Nineveh. One biblical scholar has rightly called the Assyrians the Nazis of the ancient East. Basically, people in that era wanted for Nineveh what many Americans wanted for the Nazi war criminals at Nuremberg—a fair trial followed by a good hanging! Now perhaps you can better understand (although not condone) Jonah's anger toward God.

Jonah next expressed his anger toward God with prayer: He prayed to the Lord, "O Lord, is this not what I said when I was still at home? That is why I was so quick to flee to Tarshish. I knew that You are a gracious and compassionate God, slow to anger and abounding in love, a God who relents from sending calamity. Now, O

Lord, take away my life, for it is better for me to die than to live" (Jonah 4:2-3).

The Hebrew word translated *prayed* in verse 2 means "to intervene, to interpose oneself." Knowing that God had revoked His judgment, Jonah pleads with God to have judgment restored. In doing so he reveals his motives for booking passage to Tarshish. Because he knew of the Lord's gracious and compassionate nature, Jonah had feared this merciful outcome for the wicked people of Nineveh. Verse 3 probably means, "Lord, if You stand behind Your decision for mercy, then please kill me now because I don't want to live in a world like that."

How do you think God normally responds to such flak? Some of us have been programmed by college religion classes to think of the mean, old God in the Old Testament and the gentle, nice Jesus in the New Testament. Accordingly, we may have expected the Lord to dispatch a quick lightning bolt to remove all signs of Jonah. A great voice would say, "There now, Jonah. Just what you deserve for being angry with Me." But God did not handle Jonah's anger that way. Instead He began to tenderly transform Jonah's *emotions* to help him feel what the Lord felt about those lost people of Nineveh. Are you surprised by that?

God's Process

But the Lord replied, "Have you any right to be angry?" Jonah went out and sat down at a place east of the city. There he made himself a shelter, sat in its shade, and waited to see what would happen to the city. Then the Lord God provided a vine and made it grow up over Jonah to give shade for his head to ease his discomfort, and Jonah was very happy about the vine. But at dawn the next day God provided a worm, which chewed the vine so that it withered. When the sun rose, God provided a scorching east wind, and the sun blazed on Jonah's head so that he grew faint. He wanted to die, and said, "It would be better for me to die than to live." But God said to Jonah, "Do you have a right to be angry about the vine?"

"I do," he said. "I am angry enough to die" (Jonah 4:4-9).

God's transformation process started in verse 4 with a question which can be translated, "Is it appropriate anger that you feel?" The Hebrew word "order" puts emphasis on the *rightness* of the anger rather than on the mere presence of the anger. God's question suggests that Jonah's anger found root in a selfish desire for vengeance rather than in a godly desire for justice. But Jonah maintained a stony silence as he moved to a point east of the city to wait for the Lord's answer to his prayer. Remember that Jonah had not read the fourth chapter of Jonah! As far as he knew, God might yet agree to his request and destroy Nineveh. But Jonah's unwillingness to talk about his anger did not stop the Lord's process of transformation. God's school was still in session!

Jonah probably did not realize that the Lord had provided the vine. Several kinds of vines grow very quickly in that region, so Jonah's suspicion would not have been aroused by that. Jonah responded to the pleasant shade with feelings of joy and pleasure. Since God had Jonah in a process of emotional transformation, He was helping Jonah feel about the unexpected shade of the vine the same way He had felt about the sudden repentance of Nineveh. Then God showed Jonah how judgment felt—not how it felt physically, but how it felt emotionally. The worm and the scorching east wind symbolized the onset of destruction, the very thing for which Jonah was praying. Such hot east winds, called *siroccos,* strike suddenly in the Middle East and they can increase the temperature 20 degrees in half an hour while dropping the relative humidity to near zero.

All of this aroused Jonah's anger again, as well as his desire to die. But in between these two episodes of anger toward God, Jonah had experienced feelings for a *vine* (feelings of pleasure about its life and sorrow about its death) that would now help him understand God's feelings about *people*—the people of Nineveh. So the Lord repeated the question of verse 4 in verse 9 with an important addition, "Do you have a right to be angry *about the vine?*" Jonah responded that he was so angry about the vine that he felt death was preferable to life.

God's process had run its course after accomplishing three things: (1) He had helped Jonah *feel* the gravity of death and judgment and to recoil from it; (2) He had helped Jonah identify with God's pleasurable feelings over life and His sorrowful feelings over judgment and death; (3) He had broken Jonah's irritable and angry wall of silence.

After God's tender and patient response to Jonah's anger, Jonah could now hear God's answer to such anger.

God's Answer

But the Lord said, "You have been concerned about this vine, though you did not tend it or make it grow. It sprang up overnight and died overnight. But Nineveh has more than 120,000 people who cannot tell their right hand from their left, and many cattle as well. Should I not be concerned about the great city?" (Jonah 4:10-11)

Jonah had developed a real concern for the vine in spite of the fact that he had done nothing to nurture it and had been with it for only a single day. All this feeling for a plant! By contrast, God was concerned about 120,000 people who had been objects of His love all their lives. While the Assyrians richly deserved judgment, instead, they experienced compassion from a God of compassion. In a sense, their story is the story of all of us, for we all deserve judgment—even Jonah. Jonah only saw what the Ninevites *had been,* but God considered what they *could become* through faith in Him.

Our anger toward God often occurs because we don't share His higher purpose and all-knowing perspective. If Jonah could have seen the people of Nineveh through God's eyes, he too would have rejoiced at their conversion. Jonah's anger toward the Lord arose because Jonah wanted his own will and values to prevail on earth instead of God's. Is that not the same reason we often become angry with the Lord?

I am amazed that a biblical writer admits that one time the God of the universe had a prophet who rebelled against Him in great anger. But the Bible tells the truth about life, and the truth is that every believer feels anger toward God at times. Can you admit that about yourself?

Identifying and Resolving Anger toward God

Reading the story of Jonah will do us no lasting good unless we use it to identify and resolve our own anger toward God. The human heart can go to great lengths to cover up anger toward God or to convert it into anger toward your family or others. Use these three applications to honestly evaluate your own life:

1. Presence of anger. The first step toward maturity in handling our anger toward God is to admit that at least on some occasions we *are* angry with Him. When we ask ourselves, "Why did God do that to me?" or "Why did God let that happen to me?" we are simply expressing anger toward the Lord in an indirect way. We may even fight with our mates due to anger with God. Are you willing to admit that you become angry with God at times? Can you identify your feelings of anger toward God *while they are happening?*

2. Sources of anger toward God. Many things can stimulate anger toward God, but three major causes stand out—

- extreme selfishness, such as wanting our desires to be gratified constantly *whether they serve God's kingdom or not;*
- serious losses or reversals, such as the death of a loved one, or business or marriage failures;
- unrealistic (unbiblical) expectations about what God should do for us.

Unrealistic expectations as a source of anger deserve some discussion. Whenever we expect God to do something, even though that expectation is unrealistic, we set ourselves up to feel angry with Him. The Lord will certainly fulfill every promise and prophecy in His Word, but some of us Christians have a habit of forcing the Bible to say what we want to hear. One Christian myth says, "Every promise in the Book is mine, every verse and every line." Such simplistic interpretation of God's Word brings havoc! When we wrongly think the Lord has obligated Himself to us and then He doesn't produce, we become angry.

Let me suggest a common example. Jesus says, "I will do whatever you ask in My name, so that the Son may bring glory to the Father. *You may ask Me for anything in My name, and I will do it"* (John 14:13-14). Using the passage and other similar ones for reference, several women in our church prayed in Jesus' name that a beautiful, young, airline flight attendant would be healed of cancer. Along with many Christians, they felt God had made this unlimited prayer promise *to them*. He simply *had* to heal the flight attendant. But He didn't. When she died they felt angry and bitter toward God. What went wrong?

Most conservative theologians say that such promises only *seem* unconditional; actually there are unstated conditions such as godly living. My own explanation is totally different (and you may not like it)! I believe that Jesus did express an unconditional promise, but He gave it *only to the Apostles* (the only people who were there at the time). He did this to help them carry out their crucial role in founding the church.

Whether you accept this view of prayer or not, I hope you will agree that unbiblical expectations can make us angry with God. We can set Him up to fail.

3. Resolution of anger toward God. Anger toward the Lord is *always* negative anger (even when it is predictable) because God never sins or mistreats anyone. As we discussed in chapter 3, we deal with negative anger by (1) repentance, (2) submission to God, (3) reconciliation, and (4) communication. The Lord will treat us with love even when we feel angry with Him. If you are holding angry feelings toward God, why not pray *right now* and ask His help in transforming your emotions? He did it for Jonah and He will do it for you.

A Personal Response
Study Psalms 7, 10, 13, and 22 to see how godly men have used prayer to work out their anger and other emotions toward God.

Sorrow: Pain from the Past

Americans deny sorrow more than anything except death itself. To understand why, we must look beyond the simple fact that people find sorrow unpleasant. Our Declaration of Independence speaks of our right to "life, liberty, and the pursuit of happiness." But some of us feel we have *a right to be happy,* not merely the right to pursue happiness. Sorrow treads on our assumed right to be happy.

The ancient thinkers held a different view of life. For example, the Greek biographer and moralist Plutarch wrote, "Many wise men regard life as punishment, and the birth of man especially as his greatest misfortune" (*Consolatio Ad Apollonium,* p. 27). We will probably not identify with Plutarch's grim view of life, because we have our personal freedom, relative affluence, and Christian heritage as Americans. Haven't we been shielded from many common sorrows by living in a modern, powerful nation? If you have traveled outside the U.S., you probably realize that most people on earth experience more sorrow than we do. Because we rarely experience deep sorrow, we fear it and wonder whether we will prove equal to its challenge. Sorrow scares us, so we tend to suppress it.

We Christians often try doubly hard to deny sorrow, because

some of us consider feeling sad to be a sin. (*"Sadness"* and *"sorrow"* will be used as synonyms.) Are we not obligated to show the joy of Jesus on our faces during every waking moment? If we show sorrow, someone will think we are "out of fellowship"—right? Such refusal to acknowledge sorrow makes us terrifically tense because some degree of sadness hits every human being daily. I hope to resolve this tension for you by exploring these questions:

● What is sorrow?
● What causes sorrow?
● Is it sinful to be sad?
● Can Christians avoid sorrow?
● How can we deal with sorrow?

What Is Sorrow?

Sorrow is emotional pain caused by some past sin or adversity. When you read the word *sorrow,* you probably think of the overwhelming emotion that hits when a loved one dies. But sorrow also comes in many smaller forms. You feel sad when someone makes a remark that hurts your feelings. Sorrow arises when you experience rejection, disappointment, frustration, humiliation, loss, or sickness. Sorrow can be mild, moderate, or extreme, depending upon a complex set of factors.

An analogy may help clarify the very general nature of sorrow. *Sorrow is to our emotions what pain is to our bodies.* Physical pain can be caused by a multitude of different things—headache, flu, muscle sprain, and so on. But no matter what the specific physical cause, physical pain hurts. Sorrow is the name for that pain in our emotional lives.

Sorrow involves emotional distress caused by past adversity or sin. Threats to our future can also create emotional distress, but that feeling is called *anxiety* and will be dealt with separately in chapter 8.

What Causes Sorrow?

At the end of the sixth day of creation, when everything was finished, "God saw all that He had made, and it was *very good"* (Gen. 1:31). But it didn't stay that way for long. Satan tempted, man disobeyed, and sin entered. With sin came sorrow, and it has been here ever since. Sadness finds its ultimate cause in sin and Satan.

Sin. Because of sin, our whole world steadily moves toward a state of greater disorder. Our cars don't naturally stay fixed; they break down. The kitchen floor doesn't naturally stay clean; it gets dirty. The whole physical world slides toward chaos (and some will recognize here the second law of thermodynamics). This tendency toward chaos caused by sin also works on our emotional lives and inflicts sorrow.

Paul refers to sin's effect on our world when he says that creation was "subjected to frustration" and stands in "bondage to decay" (Rom. 8:20-21). Our world has been captured and degraded by sin so that we must struggle against this "bondage to decay" each day.

Because of sin, death has also entered human experience bringing all its sorrow. "Sin entered the world through one man, and death through sin, and in this way death came to all men, because all sinned" (Rom. 5:12). Whether or not you completely understand the logic of this verse, I'm sure you can see the direct link between sin and death. Death, a major source of human sadness, may be traced directly back to sin.

Personal acts of sin, arising from the sin which indwells every human being, are another source of sadness. Jesus spoke of indwelling sin when He said:

> For from within, out of men's hearts, come evil thoughts, sexual immorality, theft, murder, adultery, greed, malice, deceit, lewdness, envy, slander, arrogance, and folly (Mark 7:21-22).

When anyone of us surrenders to indwelling sin and commits a sin, that act brings sadness to us and to others. But it brings joy to that twisted mentality who is the architect of sorrow— Satan.

Satan. Satan's personal actions to destroy men have also

brought great sorrow. Our minds immediately turn to Job, who experienced sorrow under direct attack from Satan. Jesus, whom Isaiah described as "a Man of sorrows, and familiar with suffering" (Isa. 53:3), felt sorrowful largely because of incessant attacks from the evil one.

Reluctant judgment. God's just acts of judgment against human sin have brought sadness to mankind. The writer of the Book of Lamentations wails in sorrow over God's righteous judgment upon Israel. I hasten to add that God does not want to inflict judgment and sorrow. Peter says, "He is patient with you, not wanting anyone to perish, but everyone to come to repentance" (2 Peter 3:9). Through Ezekiel, we hear God say, "I take no pleasure in the death of anyone. . . . Repent and live!" (Ezek. 18:32) But even reluctant judgment from a compassionate God brings sadness to sinful man.

In summary, sorrow flows directly from sin and Satan. I feel sorrowful just writing about it, and I'm sure you are feeling sad from reading about it. But we Christians need not despair, for Jesus said, "In this world you will have trouble. But take heart! I have overcome the world" (John 16:33).

Is It a Sin to Be Sad?

Feeling sad is not a sinful act because even God experiences sorrow. This may shock you a bit, but human sin and rebellion against the Lord bring Him emotional pain. Nothing has surprised me more in the past year of studying the Bible than to learn that God Himself is affected emotionally by human behavior. I had grown up thinking of heaven as a place where a sad word is never spoken and where there is never a cloud in the sky. But that isn't the case. In chapter 1 we discussed God's grief and pain because of the depth of man's sin (Gen. 6:5-6). Not even God has escaped the sorrow sin has brought. Why then do *we* expect freedom from it?

God experienced sadness again after redeeming Israel from Egypt. The people "rebelled" frequently against the Lord and "vexed" Him (Ps. 78:40-41).

But sin is not the only thing that causes God sorrow. Consider this verse: "When the angel stretched out his hand to destroy Jerusalem, the Lord was grieved because of the calamity and said to the angel who was afflicting the people, 'Enough! Withdraw your hand'" (2 Sam. 24:16). God suffered emotionally from His decision to send a plague and have thousands die because David had sinned. It pained God to bring judgment upon His people.

Our God is sovereign, infinite, and holy. Yet He does not live in splendid isolation like the god of deism. This god is thought to have created the world and then walked away to let it run down like a giant clock. God has chosen to involve Himself personally (and therefore emotionally) in the affairs of men. He cares about us and is affected by how we live.

Not only do we experience sorrow because of sin and Satan, but our emotional susceptibility to sadness exists because we are created in God's image, and live in a fallen world.

The New Testament provides examples of people feeling sorrowful without sin. Sorrow played a part in Paul's contact with the Corinthians (2 Cor. 12:21). Even Jesus experienced sorrow as the sinless Son of God when He cried from the cross, "My God, My God, why have You forsaken Me?" (Matt. 27:46; see also Mark 14:34; Luke 13:34)

So we conclude that simply to feel sorrowful cannot be sinful. Furthermore, sadness cannot be totally avoided by anyone—even God! In that case the next question logically follows:

How Can We Deal with Sorrow?

Use the following three applications to evaluate sorrow in your own experience.

1. Christians will experience sadness because they live in a fallen world; so the first step in dealing with sorrow is to accept it, expect it, and prepare for it. Believers should not deny the presence of emotional distress in their lives by thinking that they are beyond sorrow.

What is your reaction to these statements?
- In my church I can freely share my sadness without fear of ridicule.
- I am depending on money to protect me from sorrow.
- I thought that God had promised to spare me from sorrow, but now I know I was wrong.

In relation to this last response statement, I must confess that I have lived a comparatively sorrow-free life. No members of my immediate family have died and none are presently threatened by serious illness. I sometimes think my life will always go like this. I take for granted the peace and security God has permitted me to enjoy up to this moment. But God has *not* promised to spare me from sorrow and I must prepare for it while I can.

2. The second step in dealing with sadness is to avoid it in some areas that we can control. A great deal of sorrow is self-inflicted due to our sinful behavior (Prov. 11:8; 1:22-27). Obeying God gives us the best possible life (and the least sorrow) in a fallen world (Prov. 10:29).

Recently, I sinned and brought sorrow on myself and my daughter. I had been under an unusual degree of stress which probably contributed to the process. My four-year-old did something childish (i.e., *normal* for a child), and I yelled at her and called her a "dummy." I had never done that to her before. I could see her physically recoil when the word hit. It was like watching an artillery piece recoil after firing. Except this wasn't an army gun—it was a little child. I caused her sorrow then, and I feel sad about it still. Perhaps some area in your relationships is creating pain that could be avoided by exercising self-control.

3. When we experience sadness, our great need is for consolation. As believers we can seek consolation from the Lord and from other members of the body of Christ (see 2 Cor. 1:3-5).

- Do we reveal sorrow to our close Christian friends or do we pretend that none of us have any?

- Do we ask God to comfort us in times of sorrow or are we too proud to admit our need?

The End of Our Sorrow

You will probably greet the end of this chapter with relief because even discussing sorrow brings some pain. You can drop the *subject* of sorrow here, though not the *experience* of it. But I have good news: God will one day remove sorrow from every believer forever: "He will wipe every tear from their eyes. There will be no more death or mourning or crying or pain, for the old order of things has passed away" (Rev. 21:4).

A Personal Response

Read 2 Corinthians 7 several times (in different translations).
- Is is always wrong to cause someone to feel sorrow?
- How can this process be abused?

A Strategy for Personal Peace

If there is one thing I could use more of, it's personal peace. I'm sure it all goes back to the kind of personality I have. I feel most comfortable when things are under control. When events in my life follow predictable patterns and when I can foresee the possible consequences of my decisions, I feel at peace.

Lately, I've faced situations which I can't control and consequences which I can't foresee. These things unsettle me. For example, the elders of our church have been discussing a plan which would more than double our size and change the dynamics of our whole body. I cannot foresee or control the consequences of such a decision, so I am struggling to maintain my emotional equilibrium.

I once watched children throw a cat into the air to see him land on his feet. At times I feel like a cat who doesn't know where "down" is, and therefore doesn't know where to put his feet! Do you also struggle at times for personal peace? If so, I invite you to join me in looking at steps each of us can take to enhance our inner peace.

What Is Personal Peace?

This chapter deals with just one aspect of peace. It will not deal with peace between nations or even peace between individuals.

Understanding peace within ourselves (personal peace) will be our goal.

Peace in our English Bibles is translated from Hebrew and Greek words. In the Old Testament, the Hebrew word *shalom* is used for peace. Shalom expresses a positive and comprehensive concept of peace because shalom means "the presence of well-being," and implies completeness and wholeness. By contrast, the Greek word for peace, *eirene,* expresses a negative concept of peace because eirene means "the absence of war." What we long for is more than the absence of strife. We long for the presence of well-being within ourselves. I am happy to report that for those passages in the Old and New Testaments dealing with personal peace, the Hebrew meaning of peace dominates.

Biblical word meanings are often easier to understand if we look at words of similar meaning and words of opposite meaning used in Scripture. For *peace,* the picture looks like this:

Antonyms	Synonyms
fear	quietness
terror	confidence
trouble	rest
distress	joy
disorder	order

When we experience the emotions listed in the left-hand column, we need peace. When we feel the things in the right-hand column, we have peace.

So we arrive at this definition: *Personal peace is a feeling of confident well-being arising from reconciliation and cooperation with God.* We have explored the first half of this definition, but it's the second half that tells how we get peace.

The Foundation for Personal Peace
Personal peace can only be gained by making peace with God

through faith in Jesus Christ. On the long haul, a person cannot experience inner peace while living as an enemy of God. When someone sins, a fear of punishment rises within him, robbing him of his sense of well-being. The long-lasting effects of guilt can be illustrated by the story of a man who stole a blanket from the navy, and 35 years later sent a check to the Internal Revenue Service because he couldn't get any peace about it.

But Christians can feel real freedom from guilt because they have peace with God. Paul says, "Since we have been justified through faith, we have peace with God through our Lord Jesus Christ" (Rom. 5:1). Men can have no peace with God apart from justification and there can be no justification apart from faith in Jesus Christ. I want to stress another aspect of Romans 5:1. The use of the present tense implies continuing action—as believers, we *keep on having* peace with God.

How closely our peace is connected with Jesus can be seen by Paul's statement: "He Himself is our peace" (Eph. 2:14). The peace we have with God through Christ permeates our lives because of the Holy Spirit. After receiving the Spirit at the moment of salvation, a believer has access to the fruit of the Spirit which includes peace (Gal. 5:22).

When we have peace with God, we can experience personal peace in our emotional lives. Jesus spoke to the Apostles of this feeling of well-being in the Upper Room. Those men felt anything but peaceful. Their Lord had been threatened with death (they probably had been too), He had recently predicted His betrayal, and now He told them He was leaving them. Like condemned men eating their last meal, these men were filled with foreboding during the Last Supper.

Jesus told them, "Peace I leave with you; My peace I give you. I do not give to you as the world gives. Do not let your hearts be troubled and do not be afraid" (John 14:27). We need this peace that can only come from Jesus when we deal with trouble in our hearts. In Romans 8:5-6, Paul relates this peace to our living for God: "Those who live on the level of the Spirit have the spiritual outlook, and that is life and peace" (Rom. 8:6, JB).

Since we gain access to personal peace through faith in Christ and can sustain that feeling by obedient living, Paul can logically command us to "let the peace of Christ rule in your hearts" (Col. 3:15).

After we have peace with God and peace within ourselves, we can carry out our responsibility to live at peace with others. (This type of peace is not within the scope of this chapter, but see Romans 12:18; 14:19; James 3:18; Matthew 5:9.)

Four Principles for Personal Peace

Paul's Letter to the Philippians. Anyone who reads Paul's Letter to the Philippians can sense the upbeat tone of this Book. In fact, most commentators assert that joy is the theme of Philippians. How surprising it is to study the situation carefully and find that Paul and the Philippian believers had excellent reasons to feel troubled and distressed instead of joyful. Their joy flowed from the peace they had in adverse circumstances. We can gain a perspective on their peace and joy by looking at their actual situation.

Philippi was a city in eastern Greece named for Philip II, the father of Alexander the Great. But by Paul's time, Philippi was heavily populated with the descendants of Roman soldiers, for in 46 B.C., two Roman armies had fought with one another near Philippi. The assassination of Julius Caesar had resulted in civil war which was settled near Philippi when Brutus (you remember him!) and Cassius were defeated by Octavian and Antony (Cleopatra's boyfriend). Probably to save money, the victors had settled their army at Philippi, giving them full authority to rule the city as a Roman colony in the middle of Greece. Paul came into conflict with the Roman rulers of Philippi only a few days after arriving and making some converts. The church in Philippi experienced powerful opposition right from the start. So Paul encouraged the believers to contend "as one man for the faith of the Gospel without being frightened in any way by those who oppose you" (Phil. 1:27-28). He said, "You are going through the same struggle you saw I had [against Roman opposition], and now hear that I still have" (v. 30).

Because of the joyful tone of the letter, you might think Paul was writing from the quietness of some Christian resort, but actually he was in chains in Rome! (see Phil. 1:12-14) Paul knew that he might be executed in Rome. How could he have written such an upbeat letter from death row and how could he have expected the Philippians to live with confident well-being? He could do it because he had God's peace in the midst of crisis. So Paul's comments about peace in this letter did not come from a fog-headed expert in an ivory tower, but from a man deeply concerned about his life and that of his friends.

The first principle for personal peace—no matter what our circumstances, we can live for the Lord with the confidence that He is working within us. Paul wrote, "Continue to work out your salvation with fear and trembling for it is God who works in you to will and do what pleases Him" (Phil. 2:12-13). Paul knew that the Romans were trying to frighten these believers, but he said that the only thing to tremble about was knowing that God Himself was working within them. Paul drew peace from knowing that God actively intervenes in Christians' lives. But the Christian life does not consist of sitting back waiting for God to do it all. We have an active responsibility to live for God. That's why Paul commanded the believers, saying, "Continue to work out your salvation."

The second principle for personal peace—in situations which trouble us, we ask God for help and for a feeling of confident well-being. Prayer to our loving Father should be our automatic reaction when anxiety hits (Phil. 4:6). Paul expressed the result of such prayer by saying, "The peace of God, which transcends all understanding, will guard your hearts and your minds in Christ Jesus" (Phil. 4:7). It's not hard to see that the Philippians were feeling anxiety due to the pressure on them.

Paul's counsel may seem obvious to you, but I know what happens to me when I'm under intense pressure. I feel that I can't spare the time to pray because I'm too busy meeting the crisis. But then I think, *Barry, that's exactly why you had better pray!* It takes sheer willpower for me to stop what I'm doing and seek God's help for 30 seconds. I need God's help, but I often try to conquer my problems alone.

Before leaving Philippians 4:7, we should consider a few more of its facets. The feeling of confident well-being that we receive from God "transcends all understanding." Such a feeling cannot be rationally justified by looking at our circumstances. Recently, I skimmed a book that contained the dying words of many people and felt amazed at the profound peace evidenced by those who knew they belonged to Jesus. Certainly such peace could not be justified by their circumstances. It transcended all understanding.

The peace of God affects more than just our emotional life. Paul says it "will guard your hearts and your minds." The word *heart* means the center of the emotions and the will, while the *mind* relates to our world of thoughts. Undoubtedly, the city of Philippi, being a Roman colony in the midst of a conquered nation, had guard patrols for security purposes. So Paul wrote to these sons and daughters of Roman soldiers using the military term, *guard.* God's peace, a feeling of confident well-being, guards our emotions, wills, and thoughts, and supersedes human understanding.

The third principle for personal peace—when we face disturbing circumstances, we must guard our thought life carefully. Centering our thoughts on the negative possibilities will lead us into depression rather than peace.

We see the same balance here of human responsibility and divine enabling power that we saw in Philippians 2:12-13. The second principle tells what *God* will do to protect our inner lives while the third principle tells what *we* must do ourselves. Paul outlines the plan by saying, "Whatever is true, whatever is noble, whatever is right, whatever is pure, whatever is lovely, whatever is admirable—if anything is excellent or praise-worthy—think about such things" (Phil. 4:8). In the past I ripped this verse from its context as if it taught a principle of Christian meditation for all occasions (like the power of positive thinking). But this verse has a context which tells us the proper sphere of its use. When something threatens our well-being, we are to "think about noble, right, pure, lovely, and admirable things." This does not amount to ignoring the realities of life; after all, Paul has already mentioned the hard facts of struggle, opposition, fear, and anxiety. But to permit our minds to continually dwell on the negative possibilities is to be sucked down the drain by depression.

I find this principle easy to teach but hard to practice. Having spent the bulk of my engineering years on finding and solving problems, I have a keenly developed sense for the negative possibilities of life. I can spot problems a mile away or give you five good reasons why some new idea will flop! Many executives have trained themselves to think in this same general pattern. But Paul warns us against a loss of perspective which sets in when we think only of the negative possibilities. We must protect our thought life.

My wife Kay modeled this principle for me in the midst of some highly stressful decisions. We were struggling with some hard questions related to buying a new home: Can we afford it? How much should we offer? What if our own house doesn't sell in time? How will moving affect the children? The many negative possibilities boggled our minds and threatened us with sleepless hours. Kay decided to stop thinking about all those troubling questions and dwell on something pleasant, so she began remembering and mentally reliving the fun we had had hiking in the mountains of Colorado. In 10 minutes she was sound asleep.

The fourth principle for personal peace—it's great to know we can depend on the Spirit of God to strengthen us to meet every situation. Paul says, "I have learned the secret of being content in any and every situation, whether well-fed or hungry, whether living in plenty or in want. I can do everything through Him who gives me strength" (Phil. 4:12-13).

Once again we are dealing with a famous verse (v. 13) which appears on almost every memorization list, so that the real contextual meaning has sometimes been obscured. God is not promising to strengthen us to leap two feet over the world record for the high jump or to earn a million dollars by next Tuesday. The phrase, "I can do everything," must be understood in its context to mean, "I can face whatever comes with the confidence that God will strengthen me to withstand the trial." Remember that Paul faced the real prospect of execution. In fact, Christian tradition informs us that eventually he was executed in Rome. God promises to strengthen us in the realm of our emotions, so that we can experience contentment even in adversity.

However, I believe this assurance of divine help is based on the assumption that we are carrying out our responsibilities in the situation (see Phil. 2:12-13). I doubt that God is promising to dump supernatural contentment on Christians who are busy running away from Him. But we *can* have God's peace if we do not insist upon misery.

Applying Personal Peace

These two applicable ideas can help us to evaluate our lives:

1. Feelings of guilt can destroy personal peace. Sinful actions produce guilt which creates in us fear of punishment, fear of worthlessness, and feelings of isolation and rejection.

As believers we need not punish ourselves by clinging to guilt feelings about our past, because Christ died for us to remove our guilt. We *have* peace with God. However, guilt *feelings* still arise when we sin and this deprives us of our full inner peace. We can thus experience a maximum amount of personal peace by resisting sin and living for Christ.

2. Some Christians have embraced the idea that personal peace comes by withdrawing from responsibility and service in the body of Christ. Their goal is to "rest in Jesus" and they

justify their withdrawal from life by saying that what they are is more important to God than what they do. In contrast to this view, the Bible teaches that we can have personal peace *while living for God* and accepting our share of responsibility in the body of Christ. Faith without works is dead.

A Final Thought on Peace

Recently a believer said, "It would be easy for me to have inner peace if I didn't have so many things to worry about!" I can understand such a feeling, but what God wants for us is a sense of confident well-being in the midst of our problems, not just when our problems subside.

A Personal Response

Work through Acts 16:11-40 which tells the story of Paul's arrival at Philippi. How did Paul find peace in this turbulent situation?

7
Is Joy a Mirage?

When I hear the word *joy,* I think of Christmas. But then I recall the last few Christmas seasons and almost change my mind.

I have observed that Christmas is all-out war. First comes the shopping skirmish as we fight through the traffic to clogged stores where it's even hard to pay for purchases. Meanwhile, we must hold the budget line, which isn't easy. Then we assault the post office, standing in long lines only to be rebuffed when our package fails to meet wrapping regulations.

At night the family armies gather strength in their headquarters; or do they? These veteran forces consist of hassled husbands, hostile wives, and hopeful children. The hassled husbands have scurried about trying to erect the tree, hang the lights, and assemble the toys. The hostile wives don't feel the hassled husbands have been moving fast enough. The hopeful children anticipate getting everything they have seen on television. Doesn't this tranquil memory fill you with joy?

Christmas provides an example of a general trend in modern life. Actually, the joy Christians are to feel as they celebrate the coming of Christ comes under attack throughout the year. Joy seems as elusive as a mirage until they get a perspective on what it is and where it can be found.

What God Enjoys

God's joy is expressed by several different phrases in Scripture. Certain things "delight" and "please" Him or cause Him to "rejoice" or "be glad." Since we are created in His image, the things which give Him joy may reasonably be expected to do the same for us.

The salvation of any person brings great joy to God, as illustrated by the parables of Luke 15 (see vv. 7 and 10). The story of the lost son centers on the father whom Jesus is using to represent God. Referring to the return of his wayward son, the father says, "We *had to* celebrate and be glad" (Luke 15:32). The italicized words translate a Greek verb expressing necessity. Salvation brings compelling joy to the Lord.

The Old Testament prophet, Ezekiel, explains that the Lord rejects the idea that He takes any pleasure in the death of the wicked; rather, He is "pleased when they turn from their ways and live" (Ezek. 18:23, 32). Peter tells us that God does not want anyone to perish, but rather, everyone to come to repentance (see 2 Peter 3:9).

Righteous living by believers also pleases God. The Apostle Paul winds up his analysis of God's mercy by urging us to please the Lord with our bodily actions (Rom. 12:1). It took Paul five more chapters to outline ways we can bring joy to the Lord!

God "delights in those whose ways are blameless" (Prov. 11:20). The Hebrew word translated "blameless" doesn't mean sinless or perfect. It refers to a person who is striving to live for the Lord, not sinlessly but sincerely. God also takes pleasure in our acts of love toward other believers (Heb. 13:16).

Looking into the world's distant past and into its future also pleases God. By contemplating creation, He is able to "rejoice in His works" (Ps. 104:31). He also takes pleasure in His ultimate plans for the redeemed. When Christ reigns on earth, God will rejoice in doing good for His people and will create an environment in which they will rejoice forever along with Him (see Jer. 32:41; Isa. 65:17-19).

What People Enjoy

Being made in God's image, we can enjoy what God enjoys. This holds true particularly for believers, since in them the distorting effect of sin is being counteracted by the Holy Spirit. Those who have no personal faith in Jesus Christ seek joy primarily in temporary things because indwelling sin dominates their lives. Notice the contrasts presented in figure 6.

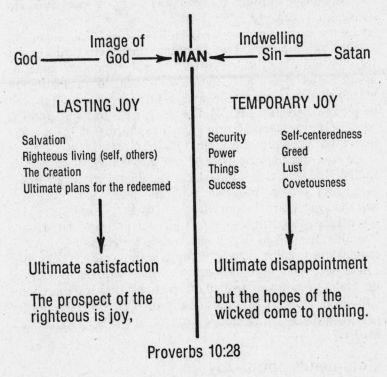

God ———— Image of God ——▶ MAN ◀—— Indwelling Sin ———— Satan

LASTING JOY

Salvation
Righteous living (self, others)
The Creation
Ultimate plans for the redeemed

Ultimate satisfaction

The prospect of the righteous is joy,

TEMPORARY JOY

Security   Self-centeredness
Power   Greed
Things   Lust
Success   Covetousness

Ultimate disappointment

but the hopes of the wicked come to nothing.

Proverbs 10:28

Figure 6

We must concentrate on those things which bring pleasure to God if we are to have lasting joy. When a person trusts Jesus Christ and lives for Him by the power of the Spirit, lasting joy results. As Christians, we can take pleasure in what God has created (see 1 Tim. 4:4), and no matter what our present circumstances are, we can anticipate what God is preparing for our eternal enjoyment.

Perhaps you were moved with joy when you heard about someone trusting Jesus Christ. And how do you feel when you hear about someone who is truly living for God? Your spontaneous joy in such things shows that you "participate in the divine nature" (2 Peter 1:4).

But our sin natures constantly pull us toward "fulfillment" in something temporary. This sin nature sucks us toward worldly security and power as substitutes for salvation and righteous living. Satan tries to get us to seek things selfishly rather than to glorify God with our possessions. Don't get me wrong; sin can be pleasurable (Heb. 11:25). But the price is too high and the "fun" soon vanishes. Heroin gives a euphoric feeling for a few hours, but then it addicts, enslaves, and destroys.

To base our joy *primarily* on our job, family, or country is foolish because these things can be shattered in an hour. Acquiring power, possessions, and success can gradually assume first place in our lives and reduce our lasting joy. Christians are not immune to these temptations. Dr. Henry Brandt once talked about his woodpile. He said, "I really enjoyed the evenings I spent before a warm, crackling fire. But I never let myself get emotionally involved with that woodpile, because I knew it was headed for the fire." How sad that Satan convinces some to get emotionally involved with temporary joy from the world, which is headed for the fire (see 2 Peter 3:10-12).

Commands about Joy

All believers must face the burden of Philippians 4:4: "Rejoice in the Lord always." Rejoicing isn't optional for Christians.

I have long been troubled by this verse because I don't always feel joyful. But finally I realized that this command relates to things I can enjoy no matter what my circumstances.

For example, I can be dying and still experience a certain element of joy because I will soon be entering the fullness of my salvation.

In other words, our lives may contain many mixed feelings because of adversity, but even then we can rejoice in *what God has done, is doing, and will do* for us. I think that's why Paul says, "Rejoice *in the Lord* always" (Phil. 4:4). At times, the "in the Lord" aspect of life may be the only pleasurable part! (See also 1 Thes. 5:16.)

Joy Defined
What God enjoys, what people enjoy, and the commands about joy combine to help us define joy. *Lasting joy is the pleasing emotion brought about by participating in what God has done, is doing, and will do.* We participate by faith as we find joy in salvation and in the Lord's ultimate plans for believers. We actively participate through righteous living and through a proper enjoyment of God's creation.

How to Be Joyful
I still perspire when I remember crossing California's Mojave Desert in the summer without air conditioning. It was like having a seat in front of a blast furnace. As I looked through the windshield on that trip, I saw a shimmering lake ahead which teased me with cool thoughts. But I drove for hours and never reached that lake because it was only a mirage. Driving longer or faster would have been useless because the "lake" had only the appearance of reality. The temporary joy offered by the world is like that "lake," slipping through our grasp and never satisfying our thirst.

The following applications can help probe your own foundation for joy.

1. Don't get hooked by the mirage of worldly "joy." Ask yourself some tough questions:
   □ What is the basis of the joy in my life?
   □ Am I setting myself up for eventual disappointment?

☐ Am I enjoying what God has done and is doing for me and for my family?

2. The key to having lasting joy is doing what God says in every area of life. Jesus said, "If you obey My commands, you will remain in My love. . . . I have told you this so that My joy may be in you and that *your joy may be complete*" (John 15:10-11). One marvelous benefit of living this way is that our children will learn to live by our example and they will be a source of our future joy.

3. Are you so busy living that you have no time to enjoy life? Why not *take* time to consider all that God has given you for your joy?

Perhaps you could make a list of some things for which to thank the Lord.

Are You Having "Real Fun"?

Last December, as my wife and I were talking, our four-year-old daughter Amy came into the room and asked, "Mommy, are we going to have *real* fun tonight?" You know what Amy thought was real fun? She wanted us to go into the living room, plug in the Christmas lights, sing Christmas carols together, and hear about Jesus coming to earth. That was "real fun" for my Amy.

We can have real fun *anytime* by participating in what God has done, is doing, and will do for us.

A Personal Response

Use figure 6 and the following verses to discover the differences between lasting and temporary joy: Acts 11:22-23; 2 John 3-4; 1 Tim. 4:4; Prov. 11:4, 7; Prov. 14:12.

8
Anxiety and a Father's Care

I really should have known better. As a college student, I always studied early and hit the sack by 11 P.M. to get a full night's sleep. Except once. My final exam in physics (worth about 60 percent of my grade) was scheduled for 9 A.M. the next morning at a lecture hall five miles away. I decided to stay up all night to patch a few holes in my preparation. At about 4:30 A.M. I leaned forward at my desk to rest my eyes a moment. The instant I shut my eyes, I fell asleep. As I sat sleeping, the clock moved on—6 A.M., 7 A.M., 8 A.M., 8:50 A.M. I sat bolt upright in my chair. Only 10 minutes remained to get to my final exam. At that moment I felt tremendous anxiety!

A big red *F* kept flashing in my mind as I grabbed my slide rule and ran out the door. Since I was not yet a Christian, I felt no qualms about threatening the world land speed record while driving over. As I collapsed into my seat, the exam papers came down my row. My anxiety didn't fully go away until I handed in my paper an hour early and reflected on how I could have slept longer.

During this experience, I got a small taste of a very bad feeling—anxiety. I wish I could tell you that anxiety is merely a vivid memory, but it isn't. I experience anxiety regularly in my profession. What makes me most anxious may surprise you—

it's anticipating preaching. You may think that's like having a quarterback flinch at the prospect of passing the ball. But about Tuesday of each week, the heavy responsibility of teaching biblical truths to 1,000 adults begins to hang over my head like a black cloud. By Thursday I sit at my desk with thousands of seemingly unrelated facts staring me in the face and I wonder if I can ever weld them into a coherent sermon. So I am strongly motivated to understand the cause and cure for anxiety. In all probability, you are too.

What Is Anxiety?

Anxiety is emotional distress caused by anticipating unknown adversity. This emotion is characterized by feelings of apprehension, worry, and uneasiness. When we feel unable or unprepared to cope with potential adversity, anxiety is intensified. Anxiety produces recognizable signs: irritability, restlessness, and the inability to relax.

My preaching schedule is a bit unusual since my first church service comes on Friday night. (Three more identical services are held on Sunday.) My family long ago learned that when I get home Friday afternoon, their best plan is to melt into the woodwork. My anxiety level rises as preaching time nears, and I become irritable. Apparently, I feel anxious because something (although I don't know *what*) could go wrong. (Please note that I am explaining my behavior and not excusing it!)

The boundary between anxiety and fear is not well defined. Perhaps we feel both emotions in many cases. I would suggest that fear corresponds to how bad things are while anxiety relates to how much worse they might get!

Anxiety must be carefully distinguished from normal and reasonable concern that our needs be met. A normal concern for our needs and those of others is biblically valid. (See 1 Cor. 12:25; Phil. 2:20-21.) But anxiety goes beyond a normal and reasonable concern for meeting needs. For example, normal concern for basic needs motivates us to work for a living; but anxiety detracts from our ability to work and may even bring us to a complete stop. With that clarification in mind, we can consider the causes of anxiety.

What Causes Anxiety?

Sin ultimately causes sorrow, an emotional distress arising from the present or past. Sin also creates tension as we anticipate the unknown future, for sin has profoundly changed our world with pressures, problems, trials, and decisions. As a result, life includes many anxieties. Jesus spoke of this situation in the Parable of the Four Sowers when He said, "The seed that fell among thorns stands for those who hear, but as they go on their way, they are choked by *life's worries,* riches and pleasures, and they do not mature" (Luke 8:14).

Personal sin also creates anxiety, even in a Christian, by causing him to anticipate punishment and alienation from God (see Ezek. 4:16-17). God has given every person a conscience which provides a limited degree of moral awareness. When a human being acts in violation of conscience, he begins to anticipate punishment (see Rom. 2:15). A Christian may have a well-educated conscience based on the standards of Scripture, but his conscience can create tremendous anxiety unless he has also understood total forgiveness through faith in Jesus Christ who took *all* our punishment on the Cross.

The lives of some Christians are pervaded by unbelief, which feeds their anxiety, letting it grow to huge proportions. Most believers find it easy to accept that God loves the world. After all, God sent Christ to die for the world and it is easy to believe He would do that for four and one half billion people. But how much harder it is to accept that God loves *them* personally!

Anxiety rises to needless levels during stressful situations when Christians forget that they have a loving Father who knows and loves them individually. Notice what Jesus said to His disciples about God's love for individuals: "Are not five sparrows sold for two pennies? Yet not one of them is forgotten by God. Indeed, the very hairs of your head are all numbered. Don't be afraid; you are worth more than many sparrows"

(Luke 12:6-7). Jesus argued from the lesser case to the greater case. The lesser case was that of the birds. Birds had such little value that five were sold for two pennies, yet God remembered every single bird.

Then Jesus moved to the greater case, His disciples. God knew each one so personally and intimately that the hairs of their heads were numbered. Jesus left the powerful punch line unstated. If God did not forget the exact situation of every bird, then certainly God would not forget the individual needs of Jesus' disciples.

Could God forget even the least of all Christians? Never! But when *they* forget about their loving Father's care, their anxiety levels can soar out of sight.

Who Experiences Anxiety?

One quick way to determine whether we always sin when feeling anxious is to determine whether God ever feels anxious. (Any emotion experienced by God cannot be sin.) Such a question seems ridiculous. What could possibly cause God anxiety? But something did. Jesus, the God-Man, suffered ultimate anxiety in Gethsemane as He anticipated the crushing personal cost of the Cross.

The Bible account of this struggle within our Lord is brief, but what it does say leaves us awed. In Mark 14 we find Jesus and His disciples crossing the Kidron Valley on their way to Gethsemane after the Last Supper. They were going there to pray. "[Jesus] took Peter, James, and John along with Him, and He *began to be deeply distressed and troubled.* 'My soul is overwhelmed with sorrow to the point of death,' He said to them" (Mark 14:33-34).

Jesus experienced such tremendous fear and anxiety in this moment that immediate death seemed possible. These profound events are so understated that the full effect of these verses escapes us. One commentator says that the Greek word translated here as "deeply distressed" refers to a person literally shaking with horror (C.E.B. Cranfield, *The Gospel According to Saint Mark,* Cambridge University Press, p. 431). Another scholar suggests that Jesus went to Gethsemane expecting heaven to open its doors as He prayed, but what opened before Him were the gates of hell (William L. Lane, *The Gospel According to Mark,* Eerdmans, p. 516). Many interpret this incident as a personal attack from Satan.

The anxiety Jesus felt in Gethsemane was expressed by the words "deeply . . . troubled" in Mark 14:33. The Greek word underlying this phrase denotes intense anxiety (Cranfield, *Saint Mark,* p. 431). During this crisis Jesus experienced anxiety, fear, and sorrow. He had to face the full cost of taking on Himself the sins of the world. Nothing could save Him from the wrath of God as He became sin on our behalf. Jesus could expect no relief from the Father as He experienced total alienation from the Father. That's why on the cross He cried, "My God, My God, why have You forsaken Me?" (Matt. 27:46) Jesus experienced ultimate anxiety in those excruciating moments.

As far as I can tell, God never personally experienced anxiety apart from those hours ending with the death of Jesus on the cross. But such a black event contains tremendous hope for us! Since Jesus has experienced ultimate anxiety, He can identify with our feelings perfectly when we begin to feel anxious. He's been there, and beyond.

We have already seen that humanity universally experiences anxiety as part of life in a fallen world. Those who have never trusted Jesus Christ have excellent reasons to be anxious. The wrath of God stands just a heartbeat away.

For Christians, anxiety often provides the surface evidence of an underlying sin—unbelief that our loving Father cares. To put it differently, anxious feelings are not sinful themselves, but are often symptoms of a deeper problem of unbelief, which is sin. (I hasten to add that some anxiety has deep roots in emotional or psychological problems requiring the help of skilled Christian counselors.)

A thoughtful reader might conclude, on the basis of what has been said, that Jesus was guilty of unbelief. But compared with the anxiety felt by Christians today, Jesus' anxiety was unique in two respects:

1. He correctly anticipated God's wrath upon Himself at the cross. Believers will never experience God's wrath since Jesus took it all upon Himself for us.

2. He recognized that He could expect no help from the Father while suffering for our sins. We believers cannot ever be separated from the care of a loving Father. For these reasons Jesus experienced anxiety quite properly and without unbelief.

Jesus Teaches about Anxiety

Jesus always confronted vital issues, and anxiety was no exception. Consider Luke 12:22-23: "Then Jesus said to His disciples: 'Therefore I tell you, do not worry about your life, what you will eat; or about your body, what you will wear. Life is more than food, and the body more than clothes.'"

Jesus was not speaking of a normal concern for the needs of life. He talked of *emotional distress* about whether basic needs would be met. But why would the disciples feel such distress about future food and clothing? Put yourself in their place and the reason for their anxiety becomes clear. The period of Jesus' wide popularity had ended. People were plotting to kill Him, and His disciples had been expelled from their synagogues and families. Those planning death for Jesus might have had similar plans for His key followers. In view of such conditions, any of us could have fallen prey to anxiety. Not even life itself was a sure thing.

As Jesus saw the anxiety building in the hearts of His disciples, He reminded them that life consisted of more than food and clothing. He urged them to look beyond pressing needs to see a loving Father who is the "more" that life holds. When Jesus dealt with the need for food, He said, "Consider the ravens; they do not sow or reap, they have no storeroom or barn; yet God feeds them. And how much more valuable you are than birds! Who of you by worrying can add a single hour to his life? Since you cannot do this very little thing, why do you worry about the rest?" (Luke 12:24-26)

These verses and the preceeding ones follow Jesus' parable about the rich fool. That wealthy farmer in Israel was anxious about a bumper crop which overwhelmed his granaries. The farmer resolved to build even larger granaries to supply his needs for years to come. In contrast, Jesus now called attention to the ravens. They didn't have a barn, but were they anxious about being fed? No, they didn't need a barn because *God fed them*. If God fed the birds, wouldn't He feed His own children?

The rich farmer envisioned years and years of life as he looked on his bursting granaries. But the voice of God said, "You fool! This very night your life will be demanded from you" (Luke 12:20). Here stood a man who had spent his life amassing wealth to protect him from life's worries, but he had never taken time to become related to God who rules this world. The farmer thought his wealth could provide for his future, but he found that anxious striving couldn't even extend his life for an hour. Jesus said that since our anxiety and striving cannot extend life by even an hour, feeling anxious is futile. We can only find security in the assurance that God will feed His own.

Jesus used flowers to illustrate how God clothes His own. He said, "Consider how the lilies grow. They do not labor or spin. Yet I tell you, not even Solomon in all his splendor was dressed like one of these. If that is how God clothes the grass of the field, which is here today and tomorrow is thrown into the fire, how much more will He clothe you, O you of little faith!" (Luke 12:27-28)

Can you imagine the color and the richness of the flowers? Flowers don't struggle to surpass the splendor of Solomon. The word *labor* in verse 27 means to struggle and anxiously strive. Did you ever see a beautiful rose and then lean down and hear it straining and groaning to look beautiful? Of course not. God freely gave the flowers beauty. Just as God feeds the birds and clothes the flowers, He will meet our needs as a loving

Father. Emotional distress about such matters is pointless.

Since Israel had few trees, the grass and flowers of the field were cut down daily to fuel cooking ovens. God even clothed flowers which briefly grew and then were thrown to the flames. How much more will He clothe His own children!

Then Jesus stuck in the knife. He addressed His anxious disciples by saying, "O you of little faith!" Lack of faith in our Father's loving care lies at the foundation of much of our anxiety.

A very safe rule is—don't imitate the world. Unbelieving people seem almost desperate to meet their needs with the things of this world. They don't have a loving Father, but we do. So our task is to trust our Father's care while we focus on His kingdom. He will undoubtedly meet our needs. Remember that Christ said, "And do not set your heart on what you will eat or drink; do not worry about it. For the pagan world runs after all such things, and your Father knows that you need them. But seek His kingdom, and these things will be given to you as well" (Luke 12:29-31).

How Can We Deal With Anxiety?

With the help of the Lord and support from friends, I am now living with far less anxiety than I have felt in the past. We share the same hope in Jesus Christ. Tomorrow can be better than today and next week better still by the active grace of God. The following applications can help us evaluate our struggles with anxiety.

1. Dealing with anxiety is not optional. Paul commands, "Do not be anxious about anything" (Phil. 4:6a). Peter gives us this command: "Cast all your anxiety on Him because He cares for you" (1 Peter 5:7). Do we face our anxiety or do we deny it because it reveals our unbelief?

2. We may need an increased awareness of our Father's active concern for us as we face life's trials and threats. (See Phil. 4:12-13; 1 Cor. 10:13; 2 Cor. 12:9-10.) Do we think frequently of the Lord's loving concern for us?

3. Prayer provides real relief from anxiety and should be our natural response the moment anxiety begins to build. Prayer expresses our faith in our Father's loving concern. (See Phil. 4:6-7.) When we are becoming anxious, do we start to pray, or sit and fret?

4. We need to let *mature* Christians share our anxiety and help us resolve it. We should find Christian friends who accept the reality of *both* life's threats *and* our Father's loving care. (Unfortunately, some Christians don't understand life very well. They act as if the trials of life don't hurt at all, but they do. So we need to find friends who accept both the reality of struggle and the reality of God's care.) A Christian counselor may be the Lord's tool to free us from anxiety.

A Dark Future but a Loving Hand

Not long ago, my whole family went camping in Colorado. We camped near Ouray in a campground called the Amphitheater, which is surrounded by sheer mountain faces. If you have ever been in the wilderness, you know that it can be very dark on moonless nights. We huddled around the campfire as the sun dropped behind the high peaks and night fell. After some stories and singing came bedtime for our three children. But before bedtime, Amy needed to use the bathroom. Now the bathroom was about 30 yards away through the pine trees in that deep, dark blackness. A stick of dynamite could not have moved Amy to that bathroom by herself. No telling what monsters might be lurking in those dark woods! Amy said, "Daddy, will you go with me and hold my hand?"

I said, "Sure, Amy." As I took her little hand, we walked together into the blackness with Amy happily singing a song to herself. She didn't have a worry in the world as long as she held my hand.

The Father deeply cares about us as we walk into the dark places of life. I do not minimize the threats and danger of life, but our Father's hand is *right there*. We must reach out by faith and take it.

Fear: A Consuming Fire

It all began when I was shopping for a new shirt. I was holding two shirts and trying to make a final decision when screams of panic interrupted my thoughts. My daughter! Running in the direction of her voice, I found Nancy with her hand stuck in a moving escalator. Her hand was wedged into the opening where the escalator handrail circles back into the machinery. I couldn't see beyond her wrist.

Fear swept over me like a huge wave. My mind was shouting, "Lord, help!" while I tried to stop the whole escalator by holding the handrail. Suddenly, the escalator stopped. I dropped to the floor to pull Nancy's hand free and tried to prepare myself for what I might see. When all five little fingers emerged intact, I went limp with relief.

In those frightening moments, I experienced not only a tremendous force of fear, but also its antidote—God's presence. We may not have to deal with such terror very often, but all of us face milder forms of fear. We are afraid when we encounter people and situations capable of hurting us.

Fear Defined

Fear is emotional distress caused by an actual and powerful threat against a person's well-being. In chapter 8 I defined anxiety as emotional pain caused by anticipating unknown adversity. Fear bears a strong resemblance to anxiety, but anxiety is more general and fear more specific. Anxiety anticipates *unknown* adversity, whereas fear is our response to an actual threat to our well-being. Anxiety is produced by possibilities still remote from us in time or space, while fear is our reaction to *immediately threatening* circumstances.

What Causes Fear?

We are usually afraid when something powerful threatens our well-being (or that of a loved one). I knew that the escalator could mangle Nancy's hand, so I was tremendously afraid. When anything has the *power* to harm us, we fear it, and the greater the power looks to us, the more fearful we will be. For example, we may fear God, people, and death because each has the ability to attack our well-being.

Fear of God. Adam and Eve enjoyed an open and joyful relationship with God before their disobedience. But after sinning they wanted to hide from God because they were "afraid" (Gen. 3:10). For the first time, they had to cope with this new emotion. Adam had not read a definition of fear, but he felt it innately as he cowered from God's holy and righteous presence.

Our fear of the Lord relates to His power to punish unbelievers and to discipline believers. John tells us that "perfect love drives out fear" (1 John 4:18). Fear of what? The immediate context identifies it as fear of punishment for sin. Jesus took our eternal punishment for sin upon Himself at the Cross and thus removed any basis for believers to expect punishment. But we are wise to fear God's discipline (Heb. 12:5-11).

Punishment and discipline differ widely. In Riyadh, the capital of Saudi Arabia, thieves are *punished* for stealing by having one of their hands cut off. In contrast, when my two-year-old son steals food from his sister's plate, I *discipline* him by spanking his hand. Punishment extracts the full price for sin, but discipline encourages a healthy regard for good conduct. Believers should hold a high respect for God's awesome power to discipline.

Fear of people. People with power are properly feared, for their acts can threaten us with sorrow and pain. A drunken driver through the power of his automobile can rob us of life. An employer can terminate our job. An acquaintance can hurt us with gossip. If you have ever received a letter from the Internal Revenue Service, you know the fear of man!

As a pastor I sometimes fear people. To preach to people about God's redeeming love comes easily, but to preach something less popular, such as fearing God, frightens me. My acceptance by the group is at stake and I don't want to be rejected.

Fear of death. Death inspires fear in us because we don't understand it and can't avoid it. Humanity has crafted cunning plans to accomplish just about everything, but there are no successful plans for avoiding death. It looms over our future as an inevitable threat.

Is Fear Sin?

Since all of us must live in a world with God, people, and death, it seems reasonable to ask whether our feelings of fear amount to sin. The answer is *no.* As in the case of many other emotions, fear is not sin but can lead to sin if not handled properly.

The foremost proof that fear does not equal sin can be found in the fear that Jesus felt as He anticipated the agony of God's wrath at the Cross. In Gethsemane, on the eve of His death, Jesus rightly feared God's punishment for man's sins (Mark 14:33). In chapter 8 we learned that Mark's description of Jesus as "deeply distressed" referred to a Person literally shaking with horror. But Jesus' fear brings us hope, because He can understand what we face when fear grips us. For this reason the writer to the Hebrews describes Jesus as our High Priest who can "sympathize with our weaknesses" (Heb. 4:15).

"Fear of man will prove to be a snare" (Prov. 29:25). This

proverb suggests that fear of man can lead to sin by encouraging disobedience to God. In the future, my children will undoubtedly face peer pressure to take drugs, to engage in premarital sex, and to do other things displeasing to the Lord. Fear of rejection by their peers or of being called "chicken" will lead to inner conflict for them. Adults face the same forces in the business environment—pressure to hide defects, cut corners, or lie. Fearing man more than God can bring tragedy.

What Does It Mean to Fear the Lord?

When the writer of the Book of Proverbs says that the fear of the Lord is the beginning of knowledge (Prov. 1:7), he places this responsibility foremost. It would be a mistake to think of fearing God in terms of the panic I felt when Nancy's hand was stuck. But these different types of fear are related by the common theme of the power to change life. The Lord calls on believers to live with a proper regard for His power; thus *to fear the Lord means to respect and be in awe of His power so that we obey Him.*

Trying to work up fear of God can be frustrating. When I was a new Christian, I read in the Bible that I was to fear the Lord, but I wasn't sure how. I can recall making sincere efforts to create a fearful emotional state within myself. But it didn't work. It was like trying to lift myself off the floor by pulling on my own belt! Only later did I realize that a true fear of the Lord comes with the gradual realization that our holy and righteous God "is a consuming fire" (Heb. 12:28-29). Some Christians think of God as being more like a comforting hot water bottle than a consuming fire.

I remember traveling to the Grand Coulee Dam in Washington when I was a boy. At that time it was the world's largest hydroelectric dam; parts of five states got their electricity from it. As I watched the water thundering down the face of the giant spillway, I could feel the ground shaking slightly under my feet. It was an awesome presence of power, and the memory of it still sends a small chill down my spine. I knew that this vast power would not hurt me, but I felt strangely awed by its presence. Fearing God feels like that.

Based on biblical evidence, I conclude that God measures our awe and respect for Him in terms of our obedience. Thus the author of Ecclesiastes sums up his whole book by saying, "Fear God and keep His commandments, for this is the whole duty of man" (Ecc. 12:13). Moses gave the same message to Israel as the people prepared to enter the Promised Land. He spoke of fearing the Lord "by keeping all His decrees and commands" (Deut. 6:2).

Paul also stressed the theme of obedience as the expression of fear of the Lord (see Phil. 2:12-13). Paul complimented these believers on their obedience in his presence, but then exhorted them to work out their salvation "with fear and trembling" in his absence. God's apostle may have left town, but God Himself had not!

Obeying God's commands in the Bible is not the end of fearing the Lord. Included is a proper response to the authorities God has placed over us:

Sphere	Authority	
World	Human government	(Rom. 13:3-4)
Home	Husband	(Eph. 5:33)
Home	Parents	(Eph. 6:1; Lev. 19:3)
Church	Elders	(Acts 20:28)
Work	Employers	(Eph. 6:5)

Scripture verifies that believers are to fear these God-ordained authorities, for each of them holds delegated power from the Lord.

Results of Fearing God

Fearing the Lord brings tremendous benefits to us believers:

A future refuge for our children	(Prov. 14:26)
Protection from calamity	(Prov. 14:27)
Lengthened life	(Prov. 10:27)

Divine protection   (Ps. 34:7)
The pressures our children face as they grow up can be counteracted by teaching them to fear the Lord. We can't expect to intercept influences which will threaten our children because we simply won't be with them most of the time. Our best hope lies in developing in them the right kind of awe for God. And we can only teach our children to fear the Lord by doing it first ourselves. Children pick up their parents' behavior far more readily than their parents' beliefs.

Learning to Fear God More and People Less

To restate, *fearing the Lord means to have respect and awe for His power so that we obey Him.* These applications will help in an evaluation of what role fear plays in our lives:

1. The fear of man. Living our faith in Christ and sharing it with others becomes more difficult when a fear of man dominates us. In conversations with non-Christians, I have sometimes restrained myself from talking about Christ, because I feared being ridiculed or rejected. I drew comfort from thinking that I did this because I didn't want to offend them with my faith in Christ. What a convenient cop-out! I should strive to be both sensitive and bold in evangelism, and even though I still feel fearful, I'll be seeking to obey God. These statements can help us rate our past experiences in witnessing for Christ:

- My faith in Christ is a well-kept secret. I "live my faith" and keep my mouth shut.
- I want to witness for Christ, but when the moment of truth comes, I'm too afraid to do it.
- I'm willing to accept being frightened as part of the price of witnessing for Christ.

Reading the above statements will give us time to think about the response we want to make in the future.

2. Fear in a crisis. As much as we hate to think about it, each of us will have some terrifying experiences. In some of these, a calm response may prevent a catastrophe. Read

Hebrews 13:5-6 and Psalm 34:7 and then respond to these statements:

- I really believe that the Lord will *never* abandon me.
- When a crisis comes, I automatically call out to God.
- I realize that God's guaranteed presence in a crisis does not mean that I'm sinning if I'm afraid.

3. *The fear of the Lord.* My biggest problem in fearing God is to realize that He is always present although I can't see Him. When I worked as a nuclear engineer, I was sometimes exposed to radiation fields. I couldn't see or feel anything, but every moment, my body was exposed to radiation damage. Signs warned me of the hidden danger and informed me of time limits for working in the area. One night a lightning bolt shut down the lights and darkness fell. Deep in the pool of water beside me, the eerie blue glow of harmful radiation appeared. The unseen radiation field was very real and I respected its presence.

As Christians, we too live in a field—the field of God's awesome presence. Though He remains unseen, He surrounds us 24 hours a day. Our "God is a consuming fire" and He commands us to respect His mighty presence.

Love: Emotion Plus

I'm sure that many people in Israel asked Jesus questions, but the question a certain scribe asked was the best of all. He asked, "Of all the commandments, which is the most important?"

Jesus responded, "Love the Lord your God with all your heart and with all your soul and with all your mind and with all your strength." Then Jesus went beyond what the scribe had asked and said, "Love your neighbor as yourself. There is no commandment greater than these" (Mark. 12:30-31). Love was frequently discussed in the first century and the great rabbis agreed with Jesus that love held a central place in the Law of Moses.

Love still reigns in our culture as a primary theme of popular thought. Most songs and novels revolve around an axis of love. Movies and magazines bombard us with images of love—generally erotic. The beautiful words "I love you" fall upon countless receptive ears every day.

I have been thinking about the things I love. I really love chocolate pie. I love camping. I really love my wife. (By the way, this list is not in priority order!) I love my country and my parents and Colorado. Should I love God the way I love chocolate pie? Or am I to love Him as I do my parents? Or as I love my wife? Suddenly, the meaning of biblical love becomes very fuzzy. We all talk about love quite freely, but do we really know what it is? *What kind of love* are we to show God and one another? To be honest, some of us talk the language of love, but we aren't quite sure what it means.

Genuine Love

John makes a profound statement when he writes, "God is love" (1 John 4:8). A surface reading of this verse may mislead the unwary, for it must not be understood as a mathematical equation, God = love. If it were, we would be forced to conclude that love = God. The latter equation would wrongly lead us to see God in a Muslim's love for Allah or an alcoholic's love for whiskey.

The true meaning of 1 John 4:8 can be expressed this way: God is a loving Person. Love begins in God's own nature; He loves because that's the kind of Person He is. To get a more complete grasp of God's character, we should recall that the Bible also says, "God is spirit" (John 4:24); "God is light" (1 John 1:5); and "God is a consuming fire" (Heb. 12:29). In light of these verses, we should avoid the erroneous view of liberal theology that God is *only* love. But love has its origin in God's loving nature.

We know that God is a loving Person, but we must still solve the problem of defining genuine love. The ancient Greeks expressed a self-gratifying, selfish kind of love (usually sexual) with the word *eros*. God manifests a love which is the opposite of eros. He expresses a self-giving love for the benefit of others. The Greeks called this kind of love *agape*. Paul describes God's relationship to man as one of *giving* rather than *getting* by saying, "He is not served by human hands as if He needed anything, because He Himself gives all men life and breath and everything else" (Acts 17:25). God does not depend upon our acts of love toward Him, but everything we have depends on His love for us. God loves by giving of Himself for the benefit of others.

We might also call God's love *spontaneous*, meaning that

His love flows naturally out from His character and is directed toward unlovely people. All of us could show spontaneous love for a beautiful baby, but how would we respond to a child throwing a tantrum? All of us were spiritually maimed from birth by sin, but God loves us anyway. The Apostle Paul describes all of us with four words: *powerless, ungodly, enemies,* and *sinners* (Rom. 5). Yet we also read, "God demonstrates His own love for us in this: while we were still sinners, Christ died for us" (Rom. 5:8). God spontaneously loves the unlovely.

Patterned after God's own nature of love, our human capacity for love shows that we retain part of God's image in spite of the defacing effects of sin. God's divine image is being restored in all Christians who are being conformed to the likeness of Christ. Accordingly, believers should be progressing in their ability to love as God loves. John expresses this by saying, "We love because He first loved us" (1 John 4:19).

Genuine love is a spontaneous desire impelling a person to self-giving for the benefit of another person. Love has a unique place among the emotions because God in His Word gives it top rank (see 1 Cor. 13:13) and because it combines emotion and action. In "spontaneous desire" we see emotion and in "self-giving," action. Genuine love is an emotion that behaves.

Distortions of Genuine Love

Satan has been distorting the things of God for a long time. Knowing that God is love, he has concentrated on distorting that love. So it really shouldn't surprise us that people are confused about genuine love because that has been Satan's project from the start.

When genuine love is distorted, the results may not all be sinful, but they fall short of the genuine love that flows from God.

When we love only the attractive or lovable, we fall short of genuine love. Love for something lovable is not necessarily bad, but it cannot substitute for genuine love. Perhaps this illustration will help. A long-neglected biblical command reads, "Greet one another with a holy kiss" (1 Cor. 16:20). Sounds like a doctrine worthy of study! But that very response leads to the problem. A kiss served as the common form of greeting in the first-century world, and it seemed especially appropriate among Christians. Chrysostom, a Turkish Christian who lived in the fourth century, complained that the Christian men of his time were restricting their holy kisses to the pretty young women of the church! We may find that amusing, but genuine love was missing there. Husbands, you may find it easy to love your wife when she looks beautiful for that special occasion, but how about when she's ill? She may feel, look, and act terrible, but in such times you have opportunity to show God's own special brand of love. Love which is directed only toward the lovely cannot meet the standard of genuine love.

Self-getting can replace self-giving and result in another distortion of genuine love. When reading or watching television, Americans are constantly encouraged toward self-indulgence—especially in sexual activity. As a God-created capacity, sexual expression within marriage can satisfy both husband and wife. The greatest opportunity for sexual satisfaction comes when each partner emphasizes self-giving by putting the other person's desires ahead of his own. What a beautiful way for genuine love to show its supremacy! But when self-getting replaces self-giving in either partner's mind, the quest for satisfaction can prove elusive and create a problem in marriage. As Christians understand and show genuine love, their marriages will become more satisfying in every area.

A third distortion of genuine love bears some resemblance to the second, but differs at the level of motivation. Sometimes, acts of love are actually motivated by selfish reasons rather than for the benefit of others. Perhaps you have known someone who was always doing things for you. At first you took it as genuine love, but in time you realized that your friendship or favor was being bought. Perhaps the other person feared you would reject him unless your relationship with him had some compensating advantages. In this kind of love which is motivated by self-benefit, what is your responsibility in the situation? You need to show genuine love by assuring such a person that you want his friendship for himself alone and not for what he can do for you. While this is a subtle distortion of genuine love, the fourth distortion is anything but subtle.

Imagine that you had a friend who claimed to love cooking. Let's also suppose you knew that this friend really spent his time reading cookbooks rather than cooking. You would soon conclude that your friend was actually in love with the *idea* of cooking rather than cooking itself. Love which does not consummate the desire with action cannot qualify as genuine love. Usually this boils down to attraction to an idea rather than genuine love. In contrast, genuine love always moves from desire to acts of self-giving for the benefit of others.

Love's Priorities and Restrictions

God has not only revealed the nature of genuine love, but also the boundaries within which we are to love Him and our neighbor. We may compare our situation to that of a football player. The player has been given certain priorities (usually related to the goal line) and restrictions (such as the sidelines marking what is out-of-bounds). To win, the football player must play according to these priorities and restrictions. Some priorities of genuine love are:

- God (Deut. 6:5)
- Self (Matt. 22:39)
- Husband or wife (Eph. 5:25; Titus 2:4)
- Children (Titus 2:4)
- People in the body of Christ (1 Peter 1:22)
- People outside the body of Christ (Rom. 13:8; Gal. 6:10).

Our first priority belongs to God: "Love the Lord your God with all your heart and with all your soul and with all your strength" (Deut. 6:5). Biblical love progresses from the inside of a person to the outside—from the emotions and will to the actions. The great verse quoted above shows this progression: The *heart* is the seat of the emotions and the will—the inner man; the *soul* is used here to refer to the whole person, a common meaning for this Hebrew word; *strength* draws attention to a person's actions.

Each of the other priorities of love could be discussed at length, but one comment will suffice. While God makes it clear that we are to love Him above all, He states with equal clarity that our love must not stop with Him. In other words, we are also to show love to those who come after God in priority. I think that explains why Jesus answered the scribe by giving not only the greatest command, but also the second ("love your neighbor as yourself"). The Greek word for *neighbor* means "one who is near." After God, the priority list moves from those nearest to those farther away.

The restrictions governing our love fall into two basic categories. First, we are forbidden to love anything that rebels against God. John describes all such things by using the phrase "the world" (see 1 John 2:16-17). We are to use the world to serve God. Second, we can never justify sin by using the excuse of "love." (See 2 Sam. 13 for a tragic case of such distorted "love.")

How to Express Genuine Love

"Be imitators of God, therefore, as dearly loved children and live a life of love" (Eph. 5:1-2). Paul follows this command with an illustration; Jesus lived a life of love by giving Himself up for us. Showing genuine love toward people is not optional for us as believers. In acts of self-giving for the benefit of others, we can obey this command and imitate God.

How to show genuine love toward God is less clear at first. But John dispels the fog by saying, "This is love for God; to obey His commands" (1 John 5:3). Our spontaneous desire here takes the form of desiring to do God's revealed will. Our self-giving consists of voluntarily carrying out our Lord's commands—we give the Lord the actions of our lives. We don't love God as we might love chocolate pie or our parents or our country. We love Him by obeying Him.

Genuine Love in Our Lives

To be able to define *love* is great, but to live it is even greater and should become our goal. These applications can help sharpen our ability to imitate God in love.

1. Lacking desire. You probably join me in wishing for a greater natural desire to love others. Is God commanding us to conjure up a feeling? I don't think so. Let me use an illustration to suggest how we can break through this impasse of lacking desire. In snow skiing we turn by shifting most of our weight to one foot. That ski soon begins to turn and the other one follows. God has designed our bodies so that one foot can never get very far from the other. Since love combines emotion (the desire) and action (the self-giving), our emphasis on self-giving can be represented by our weight on the turning leg. I believe that as we put weight on acts of self-giving toward others, our desire will naturally follow along, just as when one ski turns and the other follows. In other words, our emotions will eventually catch up with our actions; so we should show genuine love even when our desire is weak.

2. Stopping short. All of us are attracted to the *idea* of love, but we too often stop short of putting it into action. Setting one goal per week for expressing love would be a step in the right direction.

3. Sidetracking. Our world entices us daily away from living lives of genuine love toward God and men. Work and recreation should be kept within limits that will not distract us from our loving obedience toward God.

4. Parenting. Of all people, children need extra amounts of genuine love. Studies indicate that most parents really love their children, but many children don't feel loved. Could this be true of your children? An excellent resource on this subject is

How to Really Love Your Child by Ross Campbell (Victor).

A Final Word

In the winter of 1911-1912, Robert Falcon Scott led his tragic expedition to the South Pole. With him walked Captain Lawrence Oates. All in the party were near starvation and were suffering from the effects of the cold, but Oates struggled along behind on feet that were frozen and infected with gangrene. All of the men knew that Oates' deteriorating condition meant his *certain* death and that it might doom them all since they had slowed to his pace. But they never spoke of it.

At nightfall they set up the tents in a blizzard. After they had settled, Oates said, "I am going outside and may be some time." He intentionally walked away from camp, giving up his life in the blizzard so that his friends might at least have a chance to live. Captain Lawrence Oates understood the definition of genuine love and put love into action.

11
Compassion: A Heart like God's

My parents taught me many values as I was growing up, but none have surpassed the value of compassion. I remember one hot summer day with them at Bryce Canyon National Park in Utah. We had pulled off the road to take some pictures of the rugged canyon landscape. Just after we had gotten out of the car, we saw a man, a woman, and a little girl struggling toward us. Speaking with a German accent, the man begged us to give his wife and daughter some water. All three appeared near collapse from heat exhaustion and we learned they had become lost while hiking in the canyon. The man did not need to beg because my dad and mother rushed willingly to help them to our car. After drinking water and resting, the man pleaded with my parents to take his wife and daughter to the ranger station several miles away. I thought his request was strange because I knew we would never leave any of them there in their weakened condition, and we insisted that the man come with us too. They thanked us profusely at the ranger station for helping them in their distress. But how would you relate that situation to the following one?

We were in a large city when a skid row derelict approached us asking for help. We could tell at a glance that he was in distress. He asked my parents to give him money to buy some food. My dad said, "No, I won't."

Did my parents do what was right in those two cases? Did they act in a compassionate way in each situation? In your mind you may be protesting that I haven't given you all the facts. But that's the way life is—you seldom do know all the facts. As you run across people in distress, you must often make quick decisions based on what little you know. Are you going to help or not? What would God have you do in these cases? Many Christians must face such dilemmas as they feel the desire to help but experience guilt if they choose not to help. These tensions clamor for answers.

What Is Compassion?

Compassion is being moved by another person's distress and desiring to relieve it by giving crucial help. Compassion bears a strong resemblance to love which, you may remember, is a spontaneous desire impelling a person to self-giving for the benefit of another person. In essence, we can say that compassion is *a loving response to another person's distress.* Compassion embraces our emotional and behavioral response to human need. In the situation at Bryce Canyon, our whole family was emotionally moved by the physical condition of the family suffering heat exhaustion. But what we felt would have failed to qualify as compassion if we had not tried to relieve their situation by giving crucial help.

Before continuing, the vocabulary of compassion should be clarified. The word *compassion* includes action but stresses the emotion of being moved by another's distress. On the other hand, *to show mercy* or *pity* stresses the action which flows from being moved. Compassion begins with God Himself.

God's Compassion

How does God describe His character? The Lord answered that question for Moses, who wanted to know Him better (Ex. 34). God made Himself known to Moses by saying, "The Lord, the *compassionate* and gracious God . . . yet He does not leave the guilty unpunished" (Ex. 34:6-7a). I find it remarkable that

God chose to mention compassion first. God wants to respond to men in a compassionate way, but at the same time, He will punish those who prefer their rebellion over His mercy. Even God's deep compassion has limits.

Even when we sin and God disciplines us, His compassion doesn't stop. As Jeremiah looked back with tears on God's judgment upon Jerusalem, he held firmly to the certainty of God's mercy: "For men are not cast off by the Lord forever. Though He brings grief, He will show compassion, so great is His unfailing love" (Lam. 3:31-32). God, the most compassionate Person of all, did not always give men what they wanted. The Jews earnestly desired relief from His crushing judgment, but in His perfect wisdom, God withheld this relief. Occasionally, love demands discipline to produce a needed change.

God's compassionate character found its ultimate expression in sending Christ to die for mankind. As God considered sinful man, He saw the deep distress of a sin problem which man was helpless to solve. Distressed, God wanted to relieve man's need by sending crucial help. Paul said to Titus, "When the kindness and love of God our Saviour appeared, He saved us, not because of righteous things we had done, but *because of His mercy*" (Titus 3:4-5).

But willful rejection of God's compassion leads to certain judgment. The Lord speaks of those who stubbornly refuse to listen to His words when He says, "I will allow no pity or mercy or compassion to keep Me from destroying them" (Jer. 13:10, 14). For those who sin in ignorance, Paul uses his own life to illustrate that God's mercy waits for them patiently (1 Tim. 1:13). Paul did not willingly rebel against God's mercy in Jesus Christ, and God dealt with him tenderly. Thus, mercy lies at the core of God's character, but this mercy is withdrawn in the face of persistent and intentional rebellion. This balance provides the pattern for our human compassion.

Our Need to Express Compassion

Since we belong to a God of compassion, this emotion should

characterize our lives as believers. Paul writes, "As God's chosen people . . . clothe yourselves with compassion" (Col. 3:12). In fact, if someone who says he's a believer, and yet does not demonstrate compassion toward other believers in distress, there is reason to question that person's true relationship to Christ. John tells us, "If anyone has material possessions and sees his brother in need but has no *pity* on him, how can the love of God be in him?" (1 John 3:17) True compassion requires the active expression of help.

The Parable of the Compassionate Samaritan

Because of the foundational nature of compassion, Jesus made it the theme of several important parables. Jesus never taught a parable about a "good" Samaritan, but He did teach about a compassionate one. This parable can only be understood in light of its context (Luke 10:25-37).

The Trap:

On one occasion an expert in the Law stood up to test Jesus. "Teacher," he asked, "what must I do to inherit eternal life?"

"What is written in the Law?" He replied. "How do you read it?"

He answered: " 'Love the Lord your God with all your heart and with all your soul and with all your strength and with all your mind'; and, 'Love your neighbor as yourself.' "

"You have answered correctly," Jesus replied. "Do this and you will live."

But he wanted to justify himself, so he asked Jesus, "And who is my neighbor?" (Luke 10:25-29)

The setting of the story is on the road from Jerusalem to Jericho. In Luke's Gospel we have previously been told that Jesus had begun the final journey to Jerusalem (9:51). He traveled down the east bank on the Jordan River to Jericho where He started up the 17-mile road to Jerusalem. The road twists and turns as it ascends 3,300 feet, and it had been known even before Jesus' day as a haunt of robbers. Just after our parable we find Jesus at the end point of the road in Bethany near Jerusalem. Because of these facts, I believe Jesus told this story while He was actually traveling on the same road from Jerusalem to Jericho that He uses in the parable.

Jesus had many enemies and Luke tells us that the expert of religious law stood up to "test" Him. In the eleventh game of their wild match for the world chess championship, Boris Spassky lured Bobby Fischer into a long-prepared trap and gave him the worst defeat of his career. I think the lawyer was trying to lure Jesus into such a prepared trap. He began with a simple question about eternal life. As was often Jesus' custom, He asked the lawyer for his own answer. In response the man took a verse from Deuteronomy (about loving God) and a verse from Leviticus (about loving neighbors) and put them together. Where did he get such an idea? I think he got it from hearing Jesus and he repeated it as part of his scheme. Jesus predictably agreed with the lawyer's answer.

Luke tells us that this man wanted to justify himself; he wanted to maneuver Jesus into affirming that his *narrow* concept of love was good enough for eternal life. The lawyer asked, "Who is my neighbor?" He wanted to look for the fine print that would allow him to have eternal life as cheaply as possible. The lawyer wanted Jesus to reduce the broad scope of the word *neighbor*. Although his leading questions had been carefully prepared, they could not withstand Jesus' powerful answer.

The Story:

In reply Jesus said: "A man was going down from Jerusalem to Jericho, when he fell into the hands of robbers. They stripped him of his clothes, beat him and went away, leaving him half dead.

A priest happened to be going down the same road, and when he saw the man, he passed by on the other side.

So too, a Levite, when he came to the place and saw him, passed by on the other side. But a Samaritan, as he traveled, came where the man was; and when he saw him, he took pity on him. He went to him and bandaged his wounds, pouring on oil and wine. Then he put the man on his own donkey, took him to an inn and took care of him. The next day he took out two silver coins and gave them to the innkeeper. 'Look after him.' he said, 'and when I return, I will reimburse you for any extra expense you may have'" (Luke 10:30-35).

Jesus crafted a masterpiece which boiled everything down to the main issue. As Jesus and His party sat by the road (remember the lawyer "stood up"), Jesus invited them to imagine a traveler coming down the road from Jerusalem toward Jericho. We don't know if this man was a Jew, a Roman or what—he was simply a human being. The man was assaulted by robbers who stripped, beat, and abandoned him half dead. Clothes provide clues to identity, nationality, and social status, but this man had been stripped of such clues.

He lay wounded and *half* dead; that's just the kind of man we need for the story. If the man were dead, there would be no reason to stop and help him, but this man lay bleeding and dying. In just two sentences, Jesus confined the issue to that of *a human being in distress.*

Jesus asked the lawyer to envision others traveling to Jericho and coming upon the dying man. First, a priest. Who were the priests? They descended from Aaron within the tribe of Levi, and they, above all others, held responsibility for teaching the people what God is like. We have seen that God shows compassion to human beings in distress. Without any doubt the priest saw the dying man, but he began to calculate the consequences and "passed by on the other side." Did you ever wonder why the priest moved to the other side of the road? Priests lived off people's tithes of money, crops, and possessions. If a priest let even his shadow touch a corpse, he would be defiled and for a time he could not receive tithes. The wounded man could die at any moment and cause the priest considerable inconvenience.

The Levites also held ancient responsibility to represent God to the people. Like the priest, the Levite saw the dying man but moved away to avoid possible defilement.

Finally, a Samaritan encountered the dying man. The Samaritans were considered half-breeds. In 722 B.C. the Assyrians had attacked the northern kingdom, Israel, and carried over 25,000 Jews away into other regions. In their place thousands of idol-worshiping people were settled in the area which became Samaria. These pagans intermarried with the remaining Jews, which amounted to racial desecration in the eyes of the people in Judah. To add insult to injury, the Samaritans practiced idolatry and even erected their own temple to rival the Jerusalem temple. Hatred ran deep between the Jews and Samaritans.

Since the road was from Jerusalem to Jericho, in all probability the dying man was a Jew. Why should the Samaritan have helped this man who belonged to his social, religious, and political enemies? The Samaritan also risked defilement because his religion accepted the Law of Moses. But the Samaritan did not stop to run a profit analysis on the situation. He saw a human being in distress, he was moved with compassion, and he gave life-saving help.

But this compassionate man did not stop with simple prevention of death; he took steps to restore a sense of health and well-being to the wounded man. Seating the man on his own donkey, he walked the remaining miles to Jericho and then cared for the man through the night. When morning came he gave the innkeeper funds to cover about two weeks of room and board and watchful care. To cap it all off, the Samaritan bound himself by verbal contract to meet any additional expenses. He did all this *without any hope of repayment,* for Jewish courts would never press his claims. It was not the priest or the Levite but the Samaritan who demonstrated the compassionate character of God.

However, we must also consider what the Samaritan did *not* do. He did not give his entire wealth and estate to the wounded man. He did not establish an international organization to help wounded wayfarers. Some of the takeoffs (interpretations) from the parable apparently assume that he took such steps. In the normal course of life, the Samaritan came near a human being in distress and he met that one man's need with crucial help. He was looking for a way to help, not a way out.

The Trap Closes:

"Which of these three do you think was a neighbor to the man who fell into the hands of robbers?"

The expert in the Law replied, "The one who had mercy on him."

Jesus told him, "Go and do likewise" (Luke 10:36-37).

Jesus had slightly but profoundly changed the lawyer's question. The lawyer asked, "Who is my neighbor?" His question focused attention on *others* and asked whether they fit into the category of those he was obligated to love. But Jesus asked, "Who was a neighbor?" "Who behaved with love as God would have a neighbor behave?" Jesus focuses attention on *ourselves* and asks whether we have a heart to love others.

The lawyer, who had fallen into his own trap, humbly acknowledged that the man who showed mercy acted as a neighbor. Jesus told him, "Go and do likewise."

How Compassion Fits into Our Lives

Compassion is being moved by another person's distress and desiring to relieve it by giving crucial help. In learning how compassion fits into our lives, we may encounter two extremes.

The first extreme is suppressing the desire to help, a special danger for men. American culture programs men to suppress feelings of compassion. Because of this I struggle with whether or not to show compassion in my own life, for I sometimes feel it conflicts with my manhood.

In high school I had a basketball coach who had a Marine Corps background and he had brought into his coaching a little too much Marine philosophy. If a student sprained his ankle during practice, he would simply have his body dragged off to the side so that the game could go on. His favorite saying (with his hard, gruff voice) was: "When the going gets tough, the tough get going." Can't you just hear the Samaritan saying that to the dying man?

There is a place for courage and endurance under hardship. There is a place for getting up when you have been knocked down. But times can come when you are knocked down so hard that you cannot get up without help.

Some of us are tempted to rationalize our way out of showing compassion toward others. We may use one of these mental methods for *avoiding* compassion when we should be *displaying* it:

"It's none of my business."

"That's his problem; let him solve it."

"I'd like to help, but it isn't convenient right now."

"It's not smart to get involved in such things."

"They probably don't want my help anyway."

Personal Response

When I encounter someone who needs compassion, I suppress the desire to help:

☐ frequently   ☐ sometimes   ☐ seldom

A second extreme we may encounter while learning to live compassionately is not knowing when to stop helping. We will eventually run into someone who will attempt to abuse our generosity. Such a person needs our compassion, but in a different form. Two common abuses of compassion are:

1. *The dependency syndrome.* Some people think of themselves only as *objects* of compassion. They will keep taking beyond our ability to give.

In such cases real love must be discerning. Real compassion would then lead us to confront such people with their abuse of our help. Like God's compassion, *our compassion must be guided by wisdom and resistance to sin.* But be ready—such people will often try to make us feel guilty for not "helping."

2. *The big lie.* Some people will say anything to get money from you. Have you been turned away from compassionate living by people who took advantage of you? Pray for wisdom and boldness in dealing with such needy people.

Where Do We Go from Here?

In one of his most famous stories, Edgar Allan Poe tells of a man who takes revenge on a friend who had done him a minor wrong. He chains the man to the wall of a room in his wine cellar. As the prisoner looks on, he begins to build another wall of brick and mortar to seal him in forever. As the wall rises ever higher, the desperate victim screams, "For the love of God, have mercy on me!" But the wall-builder takes no notice. At last the wall is complete.

As you live your life, you will encounter people who cry out to you for mercy. Some will use real words but others will cry out silently to you: "For the love of God, have mercy on me!" Will you wall them in or help them out?

12
Living without Loneliness

Are you one of the millions of Americans who jog, take vitamins, eat low cholesterol foods, or avoid smoking *to lengthen your life?* Chances are good that you have taken one of these concrete steps to live longer. But have you taken similar, specific steps, *with the intent of lengthening your life,* to avoid loneliness? If my own church is typical, less than 5 percent of you can say Yes. The reason is simple. Few people think of loneliness as affecting their health or shortening their lives, but loneliness is killing people prematurely.

Dr. James J. Lynch of the University of Maryland School of Medicine documented the life-shortening effects of loneliness. For example, he produced data showing that *for every major cause of death* (things as diverse as heart disease, motor vehicle accidents, cancer, and homicide), men and women (ages 15— 64) who were divorced, widowed, or single had significantly higher death rates than those who were married *(The Broken Heart: The Medical Consequences of Loneliness,* Basic Books, pp. 40-41).

The strange case of sudden death in apparently healthy individuals in primitive tribes was investigated by Dr. Walter Cannon of Harvard University. In 1957 he reported that these deaths were commonly associated with intense loneliness and social isolation (Lynch, *The Broken Heart,* p. 59). More recent research confirms that this phenomenon occurs in modern cultures too.

Using such studies (some dealing with heart disease), Dr. Lynch drew this shocking conclusion: "Loneliness and isolation can literally 'break your heart'" *(The Broken Heart,* p. 8).

What is this emotion that shortens our lives? And how can we deal with it?

What Is Loneliness?

Loneliness is emotional pain caused by social or emotional isolation from intimate relationships. Loneliness includes several related feelings. First, a lonely person often feels that he does not belong (to anyone or to a certain group). He experiences a sense of alienation or foreignness. Second, loneliness can occur when he feels that others don't really understand him—that they have no empathy for his intimate concerns.

As paradoxical as it may seem, loneliness can not be equated with aloneness. Some people feel lonely even when with a group that they know. Loneliness often has more complex causes than the obvious one of being alone.

When loneliness strikes, self-pity, anger, and despair move in. In fact, two Bible personalities lead me to suspect a deep connection between loneliness and self-pity. Moses (Num. 11) and Elijah (1 Kings 18—19), two of God's greatest leaders, both experienced a crisis of loneliness, in two incidents simply oozing with self-pity, anger, and despair. Although time and again God upheld both men with miracles, they both lost their perspective and mistakenly felt God had left them to perform impossible tasks "alone." Both men cried out to God in anger and both begged Him for death. If we seek parallels here with our own times, we see that loneliness can be felt by the elite just as keenly as by the social outcasts. We call this loneliness felt by the elite, "loneliness at the top."

Loneliness: A Biblical Perspective

Genesis 2:18-25 could be said to contain the Bible's central statement about loneliness. Normally, this passage is explained by emphasizing the creation of woman or the doctrine of marriage, so you may have overlooked its value for understanding loneliness.

The Lord God said, "It is not good for the man to be alone. I will make a helper suitable for him" (Gen. 2:18).

To say that something is "not good" may sometimes mean that positive qualities are lacking. But this meaning does not apply to verse 18. The two Hebrew words translated "not good" convey the idea that it is "definitely bad" for Adam to be alone. All that God has created up to this point is good, but something is lacking that can lead to harmful consequences for man.

The word *alone* comes from a Hebrew verb meaning "to separate" or "to isolate." Adam stands isolated because he is unique in all creation. He is one of a kind. And such isolation can bring harm.

In the wake of women's liberation, the word *helper* may not have a positive connotation for some women. But surprisingly, God is the One most frequently called a "Helper" in the Old Testament. This Hebrew word speaks of a help which man cannot generate by himself.

God resolved Adam's dangerous isolation by giving him *an intimate relationship with another person.* I believe that this strategy gives us the pattern for resolving loneliness. Intimate relationships defeat loneliness. Adam had a unique opportunity to experience great intimacy with the Lord, but God did not tell Adam to resolve his need that way. He needed intimate *human* relationships as well.

Remember that God made His remark about the danger of loneliness to Himself and not to the man. Adam had not read Genesis 2! As yet he was unaware of his danger, but the Lord had a plan for that too.

"Now the Lord God had formed out of the ground all

the beasts of the field and all the birds of the air. He brought them to the man to see what he would name them; and whatever the man called each living creature, that was its name. So the man gave names to all the livestock, the birds of the air and all the beasts of the field. But for Adam no suitable helper was found" (Gen. 2:19-20).

Most commentators associate Adam's naming of the animals with the dominion God had given him over the earth. In the Hebrew mind, the power to name something implied an understanding of the thing named and authority over it. The Lord wanted Adam to study the living creatures carefully and to give them appropriate names. But I think God had a second purpose in mind. He knew that as Adam observed the members of the animal kingdom, he would realize that except for himself, male and female existed throughout creation. His great intelligence had not yet been clouded by sin. He understood. Suddenly he felt the chill of loneliness.

So the Lord God caused the man to fall into a deep sleep; and while he was sleeping, He took one of the man's ribs and closed up the place with flesh. Then the Lord God made a woman from the rib He had taken out of the man, and He brought her to the man.

The man said, "This is now bone of my bones and flesh of my flesh; she shall be called 'woman,' for she was taken out of man" (Gen. 2:21-23).

After prompting Adam's realization of his need, God lovingly met it. Just as He had brought every other created being before the man, now He brought the woman. What happened next simply defies translation. Adam's intense feeling has been buried in the little word *now*. The Hebrew translation gives the impression of an audible sign of excitement, anticipation, and relief. "At last! This is bone of *my* bones and flesh of *my* flesh!" He quickly named her *woman*. I don't think she needed his careful scrutiny, but she got it!

"For this reason a man will leave his father and mother and

be united to his wife, and they will become one flesh. The man and his wife were both naked, and they felt no shame" (Gen. 2:24-25).

From the standpoint of companionship, the parent-child relationship must give way to the husband-wife relationship. Not even the intimacy of a mother and child can rival the potential for unity between husband and wife. Apparently, this potential can best be realized at a distance from either set of parents. What this study implies is that loneliness can even strike within marriage unless each partner separates from parents and seeks closeness within the marriage.

In verse 25 the word *naked* automatically provokes sexual associations in our minds. But the flow of the passage compels us to look deeper, because sex and intimacy are not the same. The man and woman enjoyed total openness and honesty with one another without any reason for shame. Neither had a thought, emotion, or action leading to shame. Soon enough sin would shatter this picture and result in hiding, accusations, and division. Sin would give loneliness a new foothold, partially spoiling God's marvelous remedy for man's isolation. But even after sin's entry, open intimacy without shame would provide the solution to loneliness.

What Causes Loneliness?

Having gained the biblical perspective that isolation and separation cause loneliness, let's look at factors in our modern world that promote isolation.

Social isolation. This term refers to the feeling of not belonging or of not really being understood by others. I cringe with guilt when I remember my childhood. My elementary school had a very definite pecking order among the students and during the sixth grade, I was the number one rooster. Those of us at the top had firm opinions about who was "neat" and who was not. A boy named Johnny came in at the bottom. In cooperation with the other "neat" kids, I helped make Johnny miserable. We treated him like a leper. He could never belong. It was as if Johnny had some disease, and if he touched us, we had it too. So we shunned him.

I remember one camp-out with Johnny. After he went to sleep, we took all of his tent pegs out of the ground. Later, a tremendous Texas thunderstorm hit and all of us had to fight to keep our tents up. Johnny's tent, having no pegs, blew flat and he was drenched. But that wasn't enough. On the following day, we killed a rattlesnake, cut off its head, and put the body into Johnny's sleeping bag. Now you can understand why I will never be able to forget Johnny. He haunts my mind after more than 25 years because I helped inflict him with the pangs of loneliness.

Emotional isolation. A person who has withdrawn into himself because of some traumatic experience is like a castle having high walls, a deep moat, and a drawn drawbridge. He is emotionally isolated and needs human intimacy because he is lonely, yet he fears such intimacy.

Many things can cause emotional isolation. If a child is frequently ridiculed when sharing feelings and thoughts with his parents, he will soon conclude that intimacy hurts and must be avoided in the future. Parents who are cold and aloof, seldom showing love and interest, can also cause their child to become an emotionally isolated adult.

Cultural forces. So far we have considered only social and personal causes of loneliness, but cultural forces creating isolation abound. Our age throbs with the message that only weak people need others. Both God's Word and modern medical research contradict this view, but it prevails and makes us feel ashamed to admit loneliness.

A spirit of independence and competition also drives people apart. "Do your own thing" is the rule of the day. So books bearing titles like *Looking Out for #1* direct people down the lonely road of domination and *self*-fulfillment. Secular thinkers call our time "The Me Generation." Under these principles others can enjoy intimacy with us only by adapting themselves to our goals.

Isolation also occurs due to high family mobility. In large American cities, lifelong residents are becoming hard to find. Rootlessness caused by frequent moves has provided added motivation for people to trace and document their family roots. In part, this rapid flow of people occurs because career interests have taken priority over close relationships. They usually move when the company says to, no matter what the toll in intimate relationships.

Marital status. Over 17 million children in America now live with only one parent. The ranks of the divorced and the single grow larger each year. Such numerical overkill obscures the individual loneliness which is involved. Loneliness cannot be counted—only felt.

Typical Responses to Loneliness

Denial is probably the most typical response to loneliness Since many people are ashamed to be lonely, and since they are following the cultural rules, they suffer in silence and try to keep struggling forward. It doesn't work.

Some lonely people withdraw further into themselves. They may be caught in a cycle of self-pity, anger, and despair. Others may panic and jump quickly into marriage or simply into extramarital affairs, but this usually leads to deeper sense of loneliness.

Effective Responses to Loneliness

We have already learned that an effective response to loneliness is to seek intimate relationships. Even if you seldom experience loneliness, I would encourage you to implement the strategy discussed in this section. In engineering, we called it "increasing your margin of safety."

1. We can first enjoy companionship with the Lord who *never* abandons us. The writer to the Hebrews quotes God's great promise to believers: "Never will I leave you; never will I forsake you" (Heb. 13:5). This verse could not be stated more strongly in the Greek text. There are actually *three* Greek

negatives which are summed into the single English word *never*.

With God, we find an intimate relationship to which we can always turn. God never forsakes His own. When loneliness next strikes, we need to analyze how frequently we are thinking of God's presence with us. Many Christians believe intellectually that they *belong* to God, but feeling that God really *understands* and *cares* about their deepest desires and fears comes less easily.

While every believer has opportunity for closeness with the Lord, the just-me-and-God approach to life has no support in the Bible. Remember that God provided Adam with *human* companionship to relieve his loneliness.

2. Before we can experience real intimacy with others, we may need to make personal changes. We need to ask ourselves, "Am I willing to take genuine interest in others? Am I willing to risk pain by asking a mature acquaintance or counselor about my inability to make intimate relationships?"

The answer to that last question can bring an end to our social isolation, but discussion of that subject can really hurt. Some of us know that we have problems establishing intimacy with others, but it seems easier to grit our teeth and be lonely. To be honest, hearing the truth and making changes will hurt, but it will also lengthen and enrich our lives.

3. We can influence our children toward either loneliness or intimate relationships. Try these steps for defeating loneliness in your children's futures:

- Spend time with them (talking, playing, hobbies). I hope you have not adopted the idea that *quality* of time with children has greater importance than *quantity*. Fathers, we have a real time-challenge here. Children learn first from their parents how to make close relationships and then they learn what happens in them.

- Be sensitive to their thoughts and feelings. Don't ridicule them.

- Help them make friends. They need to learn how to make friends with their peers.

A Support System

Loneliness can be dealt with. God has given us a support system in Himself, our family, and other believers.

I vividly remember arriving in Washington, D.C. to begin work with the Atomic Energy Commission. My fiancée and all my friends were back in Texas. On Sunday I drove to a church where I knew no one. Even though I am generally a self-assured person, I felt very small and alone that morning. Just seconds after I entered, a man about 25 years my senior introduced himself and his wife. Percy and Alice invited me over after church to have lunch and spend the afternoon. When I arrived at church one week later, Percy met me and insisted that I come over again.

It didn't take me long to choose a church because one man jumped across a generation gap to help a lonely person. That's what a support system is all about!

A Personal Response

Study how loneliness struck Moses in Numbers 11 and Elijah in 1 Kings 18—19. What lessons emerge here?

13
Someone Close

When things get rough in my ministry, I sometimes think about finding a quiet little church nestled against the Rocky Mountains. But then I think of leaving my friends and promptly forget the whole thing.

Friends have not always meant so much to me. In fact, for about 20 years I had no truly deep friendships. Yet for over 10 of those years, I was a committed, growing believer. During much of this time, I enjoyed a wonderful and happy marriage, but here too I built subtle barriers to intimacy. How could I have lived like a lone wolf in the *"family* of God," "the *body* of Christ," and the *"one flesh"* closeness of marriage? My problem was partly biblical and partly personal.

The Bible and Relationships
Personal faith in Jesus Christ relates a Christian to every other Christian. Paul says, "In Christ we who are many form one body, and each member belongs to all the others" (Rom. 12:5). Paul makes an analogy between the physical body and the spiritual body of Christ and asserts that a vital relationship exists among Christians. When he says that each one of us "belongs to all the others," Paul gives us American believers a hard pill to swallow. Our culture stresses that we belong to

ourselves and demands that we exercise our *individual* rights. In contrast, the Apostle Paul says we belong to others and snubs the idea of individualism.

Relationship implies responsibility. Our hearts and our lungs have a physical relationship and mutual responsibilities. Without blood flow our hearts would soon stop; without oxygen our lungs would soon gasp. Similar responsibilities among us believers are frequently emphasized in the New Testament. Jesus defined our overarching obligation on His last night before the Crucifixion. He commanded His disciples to love one another.

"One another" commands are expressed about 60 times in the New Testament, the most frequent being to "love one another." John goes so far as to say, "Anyone who does not love remains in death" (1 John 3:14). John means that such a person is not really a Christian at all! The many "one another" commands (such as "serve one another," "bear one another's burdens," "admonish one another,") are specific ways of loving one another (see Gene Getz, *Building Up One Another,* Victor).

I feel safe in saying that the command to admonish one another (Rom. 15:14; Heb. 10:24) is seldom obeyed. Believers naturally gravitate to the more pleasant and comfortable aspects of love. The Greek word expressing admonition, *parakaleo,* can bear many related meanings: to admonish, warn, urge, exhort, instruct, or teach. But the root meaning involves going to someone to correct his thinking and his behavior. I have isolated this command for special mention because an expression of emotions will doubtless occur if we admonish another believer.

To share so vitally in each other's lives includes sharing in each other's emotions as well. The nature of our humanity demands such a conclusion. God created us in His image to have emotions (see chapter 1), so to exclude them from our relationships is to limit our obedience to God's commands. How else can we understand Paul's words in Rom. 12:15:

"Rejoice with those who rejoice; mourn with those who mourn"? Emotions are part of the shared experience of life. In 2 Corinthians 2, Paul speaks of grief and sorrow caused by a case of church discipline. Then he instructed the church to forgive and comfort the guilty man "so that he will not be overwhelmed by excessive sorrow" (2 Cor. 2:7). Such concern for one another's feelings should become a way of life for all believers.

When God's Word lays out so many commands, we believers begin to sink lower and lower in our chairs as the workload engulfs us. Our minds picture *endless* ranks of Christians for whom we are now responsible. And then we angrily conclude, "God's being unreasonable. So I know what I'll do—I'll just skip it!" But whenever God commands something, He doesn't do it just to give us busywork. He has a reason for it. For example, in chapter 2 we learned that God's command to resolve our anger protects us from possible depression. We may not always know God's reasons, but in the case of the "one another" commands, we can make an educated guess.

God expects us to fulfill our responsibilities primarily within the circle of people who are our Christian friends. He knows we will not have opportunity to show acts of love to every living Christian, but He certainly expects it within our circle of friends. Within the context of friendships, our emotions should find loving expression.

Friendship

What friendship is can best be clarified by several verses from Proverbs. "A man of many companions may come to ruin, but there is a friend who sticks closer than a brother" (Prov. 18:24). Dr. Harry Chapman, a psychiatrist, writes of a Kansas City surgeon who had a back-slapping acquaintance with over 300 other doctors (*It's All Arranged,* G. P. Putnam's Sons, p. 35). He made it a point to know two basic facts about each physician. But soon each man realized that the back-slapper did not really know or want to know any of them. He merely wanted them to remember him for surgery referrals. The doctors resented his pretense of interest in them.

Even large numbers of surface relationships cannot replace deep ones. It's quite possible for us to have many acquaintances—people whom we know by name. But when a crisis comes into our lives, such people will be unlikely to get involved. On the other hand, "there is a friend who sticks closer than a brother." The writer of Proverbs also says, "A friend loves at all times, and a brother is born for adversity" (Prov. 17:17).

But friends do more than provide support and companionship. "As iron sharpens iron, so one man sharpens another" (Prov. 27:17). The last clause could be literally translated "so one man sharpens his friend." Admonishing our friends has a constructive purpose. In fact, people who never admonish us might not qualify biblically as friends! Before you react to that statement, consider this: "The kisses of an enemy may be profuse, but faithful are the wounds of a friend" (Prov. 27:6). Friends may sometimes say things that bring discomfort, but such "wounds" may do us far more good than the flattery and shallowness that pervade so many relationships. A true friend will speak the truth in love (see Eph. 4:15).

One caution, however, must be stressed: "A righteous man is *cautious in friendship,* but the way of the wicked leads them astray" (Prov. 12:26). We must use wisdom in selecting those who will be our close friends, avoiding deep friendships with those who have no fear of God.

We all need friends, but most of us do *not* need more acquaintances. What we need are a few deep friendships in which we can share our thoughts and feelings with complete honesty and love. Such relationships must be carefully chosen and nurtured. For greatest value, these deeper friendships should be made with others in the body of Christ.

Finding "Someone Close"

Using the following outline, evaluate your own network of

relationships and then set some goals! Think particularly of
relationships with believers.

Level 1 • I have _____ acquaintances (people I can call by
name and who know my name as well).

Level 2 • I have _____ social friendships (people who are in
my home two or three times a year).

Level 3 • I have _____ close friendships (people who know
me *intimately* and with whom I could share *anything* without fear of being rejected).

Far too many people would honestly have to write a zero in
that last blank. Your husband or wife may not even qualify as a
close friend if your communication of emotions and deep needs
is lacking. Obviously, time will permit close friendships with
only a small number of people.

Barriers to Friendship

People who don't have any close friendships usually have good
reasons. For example, children who grow up with poor
relationships to their parents are deeply branded with this idea:
Don't have close relationships because you will be badly hurt if
you do. Such people feel fearful about any kind of intimacy.
They may also have little practical knowledge about how to
make friends even if they desired to do so. But God's grace and
the love of believers can overcome such barriers to intimacy.

Other barriers to friendship may be fear of rejection, fear of
involvement, or fear of being hurt. Few of us can tolerate the
thought of initiating a friendship and having the door shut in
our faces. On the other hand, we may fear that a developing
relationship will make demands on us which we are not ready
to satisfy. Also, close friendships always involve some pain;
what if we can't take it?

Fear is a major barrier to establishing deeper friendships.
But people don't feel free to admit fear, so the most frequent
reason given for having few friendships is lack of time.

I often see Christian parents giving almost obsessive attention to activities for their children. Certainly, it is important to

love our children and help them to develop. But some of us parents find ourselves so involved in soccer, football, scouting, gymnastics, piano, and many other *good* things for our children that we don't have enough time for our friendships. The *good* can become the enemy of the *best*. What if our children never learn to form close friendships because they never saw us do it? Will soccer fill the holes in their hearts?

Cultural patterns can also form a barrier when we try to be friends with others. At the present time, secular philosophy tells us to do our own thing and never to try and influence others. It's also taboo to let anyone know we have weaknesses or anxieties or needs for friendships. These concepts have infiltrated the church in spite of the Bible's encouragement to develop friendships in Christ. We need to evaluate whether we've been thinking more like the world than like Christ in this area, and whether we're willing to risk living outside of this cultural pattern to do God's will.

A Final Word
Over the past two years, I have gained the most meaningful friendships I have ever had. My close friends have helped me discover my emotions and grow spiritually after years of wondering why God wasn't doing more in my life. The journey isn't over yet; but through this experience, my wife and I have enjoyed greater intimacy and oneness than ever before.

Appendix

Biblical Definitions of Nine Emotions

Anger. An inclination toward aggressive behavior against oneself or others, provoked by one's indwelling sin or by the sin of others.

Anxiety. Emotional distress caused by anticipating unknown adversity.

Compassion. Being moved by another person's distress so that one desires to relieve it by giving crucial help.

Fear. Emotional distress caused by an actual and powerful threat against a person's well-being.

Joy. The pleasing emotion brought about by participating in what God has done, is doing, and will do.

Loneliness. Emotional pain caused by social or emotional isolation from intimate relationships.

Love. A spontaneous desire impelling a person to self-giving for the benefit of another person.

Peace. A feeling of confident well-being arising from reconciliation and cooperation with God.

Sorrow. Emotional pain caused by some past sin or adversity.